# TORAH PORTIONS FOR CHILDREN
# D'varim
## BOOK 5: DEUTERONOMY

NATALEE HENRY & YEVGENIYA CALENDRILLO

# TORAH PORTIONS FOR CHILDREN

# D'varim

## BOOK 5: DEUTERONOMY

Natalee Henry & Yevgeniya Calendrillo

Copyright © Natalee Henry & Yevgeniya Calendrillo, 2024.

Printed in the United States 2023.

All rights reserved. This book may not be copied or reprinted for commercial gain or profit. No portion of this book may be reproduced, stored in a retrieval system, transmitted in any form or by any means electronic, mechanical photocopy, recording, or any other except brief quotations in printed reviews, without the prior permission of the Authors and the Publisher. Rights for publishing this book in other languages are to be in written permission by Natalee Henry and Yevgeniya Calendrillo.

Unless otherwise stated, scripture References are from the New American Standard Bible (NASB), and the Tree of Life Version.

This book is a part of the Torah for Children Curriculum. www.torah4children.net

ISBN: 978-1-66640-579-8

Acknowledgments

Thanks to Ken & Lisa Albin, and our Family and Tribe at Save The Nations for your continued love, support, and encouragement throughout our writing journey.

Special thanks to Kiwi Gomes for editing and proofreading, and all the teachers at Save The Nations who have been serving in the children's ministry teaching this curriculum.

## Torah Portion Titles

1. D'varim - Words                               Page 1
2. Va'etchanan - I Pleaded                       Page 16
3. Ekev - Because                                Page 33
4. Re'eh - See                                   Page 53
5. Shoftim - Judges                              Page 71
6. Ki Tetze - When You Go Out                    Page 88
7. Ki Tavo - When You Come                       Page 108
8. Nitzavim - Standing*                          Page 124
9. Vayelech - He Went*                           Page 124
10. Ha'azinu - Hear                              Page 141
11. Vezot Ha'Bracha - This is the Blessing       Page 158

About the Authors                                Page 176
About the Book                                   Page 178

\* Indicates that two Torah Portions are combined

# NOTE TO TEACHERS/PARENTS:

Dear Teachers and Parents,

Thank you for choosing to help us equip our children in the Torah Way of the Messiah. We are grateful for you and your time of service.

Each lesson is designed as a guide for teaching the Torah Portions. We encourage you to review the lesson in advance to become familiar with the material provided and allow the Holy Spirit to give you insights for teaching the lesson.

Each lesson is structured so our children will learn from the Torah Portions, and see the connection with Yeshua (Jesus), and the work of the Holy Spirit. Our aim is not just to give information but to teach Torah principles and demonstrate how to use them in their lives.

Every lesson has a general summary of the Torah Portion for the teachers and a lesson summary for the main lesson you will teach for the Torah Portion. With each lesson, there are practical applications and questions. The questions are given at the end of the lesson, however, the teacher can incorporate the questions at any time during the lesson. The practical applications are a great way for the children to make the connection between Torah and their everyday lives.

We have incorporated learning Hebrew with the lesson in video format. Please see the class schedule.

Thanks again for your time and service in helping to equip our children in the Torah Way of the Messiah.

# SUGGESTED CLASS SCHEDULE

Welcome

Practical Application Follow-up from the Last Lesson in Book 1 *(See the Practical Application Page)*

Torah Portion Lesson

Bathroom Break

Crafts

Snacks

# LESSON CONTENTS

Torah Portion Name and Meaning
Torah Portion Theme
Torah Portion Outline
Lesson
    Title & Meaning
    Scriptures
    Theme
    Summary
    Lesson Discussion
    Turning Point *(THIS SECTION IS FOR CHILDREN 9 AND OLDER)*
Practical Applications
Questions and Answer Sheet
Crafts and Instructions

# D'varim
## "Words"

# Torah Portion 44: D'varim

The Title of this week's Torah Portion is D'varim. It is the Hebrew word translated as **"words."** It is found in the first verse of our Torah reading.

## Deuteronomy 1:1
These are the **words** which Moses spoke to all Israel across the Jordan in the wilderness, in the Arabah opposite Suph, between Paran and Tophel and Laban and Hazeroth and Dizahab.

## Scripture Readings:
Deuteronomy 1:1-3:22, Isaiah 1:1-27,
Matthew 24:1-22, Psalm 137

## The Theme of the Torah Portion:

The Lord is with you

## Scripture for Theme

## Deuteronomy 3: 22

Do not fear them, for the Lord your God is the one fighting for you.'

# Torah Portion Outline

- The Command to Enter Canaan, **Deuteronomy 1:1-8**
- Moses tells the History of the Tribal Leaders, **Deuteronomy 1:9-33**
- When the Children of Israel Refused to Enter the Promised Land, **Deuteronomy 1:34-46**
- Do not Provoke Your Brother, Esau, **Deuteronomy 2:1-9**
- Do Not Harrash Moab, **Deuteronomy 2:10-12**
- Time to Possess the Land, **Deuteronomy 2:13-23**
- Israel Defeated Kings, **Deuteronomy 2:24-37-3:1-17**
- The Charge to Reuben, Gad, and half-tribe of Manasseh, **Deuteronomy 3:18-20**
- Moses command to Joshua, **Deuteronomy 3:21-22**

# LESSON SUMMARY

In this week's Torah Portion, Moses speaks the words of Adonia to the second generation of the children of Israel who were about to enter the promised land. He reminds them about their fathers' rebellion and the punishment they suffered for not obeying Adonai's command to go and possess the land of Canaan. Moses retells their journey as Adonai brought them out of Egypt, and all the kings that they defeated by the power of Adonai. He also spoke to them about the land east of the Jordan that was divided as an inheritance for the sons of Reuben, Gad, and the half-tribe of Manasseh. Moses reminded the sons of Reuben, Gad, and the half-tribe of Manasseh of Adonai's command; "Then I (Moses) commanded you at that time, saying, 'The Lord your God has given you this land to possess it; all you valiant men shall cross over armed before your brothers, the sons of Israel'" (Deuteronomy 3:18).

The children of Israel were about to begin a new journey. This journey was to take them into the promised land. It was in the fortieth (40th) year, on the first day of the eleventh (11th) month that Moses spoke to the children of Israel of all that Adonai commanded him to give them. At this point in their journey, everyone who rebelled against the Lord when He commanded them to go and possess the land had perished, only their children survived as Adonai had promised. Caleb the son of Jephunuh and Joshua son of Nun, because they were faithful to Adonai, would also enter the promised land.

As Moses declared the words of Adonai to the children of Israel he reminded them and charged Joshua; "Do not fear, for the Lord your God is the one fighting for you" (Deuteronomy 3:22).

## LESSON DISCUSSION

## THE WORD REQUIRES OBEDIENCE

### Deuteronomy 1:1-5 NASB

"These are the words which Moses spoke to all Israel across the Jordan in the wilderness, in the Arabah opposite Suph, between Paran and Tophel and Laban and Hazeroth and Dizahab. **2** It is eleven days' journey from Horeb by the way of Mount Seir to Kadesh-Barnea. **3** In the fortieth year, on the first day of the eleventh month, Moses spoke to the children of Israel, according to all that the Lord had commanded him to give to them, after he had defeated Sihon the king of the Amorites, who lived in Heshbon, and Og the king of Bashan, who lived in Ashtaroth and Edrei. **5** Across the Jordan in the land of Moab, Moses undertook to expound this law, saying,"

As the children of Israel were about to go into the promised land, one would think that Moses would have some great words of inspiration and encouragement to share with them, yet instead, he began with the rebellion that explained to them how they arrived at their current location east of the Jordan. He told them everything God had commanded him about them. Moses even reminded them about the sons of Esau and the sons of Lot who possessed their lands even though the inhabitants were greater than they were. Every commandant that Adonai gave to the children of Israel (the parents) Moses also spoke to the second generation.

**Why was the word Moses spoke to the children of Israel important?**

1. Adonai is faithful to keep His promise. Deuteronomy 1:10-11, Deuteronomy 3:1-3.

**Deuteronomy 2:18-22**

'Today you shall cross over Ar, the border of Moab. **19** When you come opposite the sons of Ammon, do not harass them nor provoke them, for I will not give you any of the land of the sons of Ammon as a possession, because I have given it to the sons of Lot as a possession.' **20** (It is also regarded as the land of the Rephaim, for Rephaim formerly lived in it, but the Ammonites call them Zamzummin, **21** a people as great, numerous, and tall as the Anakim, but the Lord destroyed them before them. And they dispossessed them and settled in their place, **22** just as He did for the sons of Esau, who live in Seir, when He destroyed the Horites from before them; they dispossessed them and settled in their place even to this day.

2. Every generation is responsible to follow and obey the commandments (words) of Adonai. Only when we obey will we receive His promises.

**Deuteronomy 3:18-22**

"Then I commanded you at that time, saying, 'The Lord your God has given you this land to possess it; all you valiant men shall cross over armed before your brothers, the sons of Israel. **19** But your wives and your little ones and your livestock (I know that you have much livestock) shall remain in your cities which I have given you, **20** until the Lord gives rest to your fellow countrymen as to you, and they also possess the land which the Lord your God will give them beyond the Jordan. Then you may return every man to his possession which I have given you.'
**21** I commanded Joshua at that time, saying, 'Your eyes have seen all that the Lord your God has done to these two kings; so the Lord shall do to all the kingdoms into which you are about to cross. **22** Do not fear them, for the Lord your God is the one fighting for you.'

3. It was a warning to the children so they would not follow in their parents' rebellion.

### Hebrews 3:7-11

Therefore, just as the Ruach ha-Kodesh says, "Today if you hear His voice, **8** do not harden your hearts as in the rebellion, on the day of testing in the wilderness. **9** There your fathers put Me to the test, though they saw My works for forty years. **10** Therefore I was provoked by this generation, and I said, 'They always go astray in their heart, and they have not known My ways.'
**11** As I swore in my wrath, 'They shall not enter My rest.'"

**As believers in Yeshua, we are responsible for obeying the words of Adonai, just as the children of Israel were.** John 15:7-10

### John 15:10

If you keep My commandments, you will abide in My love, just as I have kept My Father's commandments and abide in His love.

## TURNING POINT:

## PERSPECTIVE: GRASSHOPPER OR WARRIOR?

The children of Israel were afraid to go and conquer the land of Canaan which Adonai had given them because they saw giants in the land. In this week's Torah portion, we learn that the land that Adonai gave to the sons of Esau and the sons of Lot also had giants in it before they possessed the land. They conquered its inhabitants and possessed the land because Adonai went before them and fought for them just as He had promised to do for the children of Israel.

What was the difference between Lot's and Esau's descendants, and the children of Israel? The children of Israel were fearful, they did not trust Adonai's word, and they saw themselves as grasshoppers. Their perspective (how they saw themselves) was different from what the word of Adonai declared about them. They were God's treasure and a nation of kings and priests (Exodus 19:5-6). Esau's and Lot's descendants went out as warriors.

Moses constantly reminded the children of Israel not to fear, because Adonai, your God, goes before you. They had to learn to obey the Word of Adonai instead of their fears. The second generation of the children of Israel led by Joshua, were warriors who conquered kings and possessed their inheritance. They obeyed the word of Adonai. Like the children of Israel, we too have to learn to obey the Word of God and not our fears, for He goes before us to protect and to fight for us.

**Are you a warrior or a grasshopper in your generation?**

## PRACTICAL APPLICATIONS
DECLARING THE WORD

### FOR CHILDREN 4-6 YEARS OLD
Parents, please read Psalm 119:1-16 as a declaration over your child/children.

### FOR CHILDREN 7-12 YEARS OLD
Parents, please read Psalm 119:1-16 as a declaration over your child/children.

Children, please read two verses each night before bed from Psalm 119:1-16.

### FOLLOW-UP FROM THE LAST TORAH PORTION
Ask who wants to share from last week's practical application Taking Responsibility for Your Actions?

### FOR CHILDREN 4-6 YEARS OLD
If you get in trouble this week don't try to make excuses for your actions. Admit you're wrong and ask for forgiveness.

### FOR CHILDREN 7-12 YEARS OLD
When you do something that is not acceptable to your parents or teachers, don't try to explain or make excuses for your actions. Admit you're wrong and ask for forgiveness.

When your friend asks you to do something. Do not make a promise if you are not able to keep your promise. Always ask your parent's permission before making a promise to a friend.

# QUESTIONS - TEACHERS ANSWER KEY

1. **How many days journey is it from Mount Seir to Kadeh-Barnea?**
   Eleven (11) days

2. **In Which year of the journey did Moses declare the word of Adonai to the second generation?**
   Fortieth (40th) year

3. **Which two relatives did Adonai tell the children of Israel not to disturb when they passed through their land?**
   Sons of Esau and sons of Lot

4. **Which king was defeated in Heshban?**
   Sihon

5. **Who was the defeated king of Bashan?**
   Og

6. **Who settled in Mount Seir?**
   Esau

7. **Who were the two men who did not perish in the wilderness?**
   Caleb and Joshua

8. **In what land were they when Moses declared the word of Adonai?**
   Moab

9. **What day and month was it?**
   First day of the eleventh (11th) month

10. **Why did Adoani tell the children of Israel not to disturb the sons of Esau or Lot?**
    He had already given the land to them as their possession

**QUESTIONS - CHILDREN'S COPY**

1. How many days journey is it from Mount Seir to Kadeh-Barnea?

2. In Which year of the journey did Moses declare the word of Adonai to the second generation?

3. Which two relatives did Adonai tell the children of Israel not to disturb when they passed through their land?

4. Which king was defeated in Heshban?

5. Who was the defeated king of Bashan?

6. Who settled in Mount Seir?

7. Who were the two men that did not perish in the wilderness?

8. In what land were they when Moses declared the word of Adonai?

9. What day and month was it?

10. Why did Adoani tell the children of Israel not to disturb the sons of Esau or Lot?

## CRAFTS SUPPLIES FOR TORAH PORTION D'VARIM

**SUPPLIES:**
1. "12x12" BLACK Cardstock
2. White Marker
3. Star Stickers
4. Glitter Glue
5. Gold and Silver Cardstock
6. Gems
7. Glue Sticks
8. Plain Print Paper
9. Markers, Pencils, or Crayons

**CRAFTS: STARS OF HEAVEN**:

1. On the black cardstock, place gold and silver star stickers. Then draw the outline of stars with the white markers.

2. Fill in the white stars with various glitter glue colors. Be careful now. Try not to touch it, so it dries well.

3. Put dots around with a glitter glue gun. Also work carefully around it, allowing it to dry.

4. With a glue stick, paste gold and silver stars made from cardstock.
5. Finish the starry sky with gems.

6. Color in the graffiti header "Devarim", sketched by classic graffiti artist, *Joel Calendrillo*.

7. Label with a white marker the verse corresponding to this activity: Deuteronomy 1:10

FINAL WORK

# Va'etchanan

## "I Pleaded"

# Torah Portion 45: Va'etchanan

The title of this week's Torah Portion is Va'etchanan which means **"I pleaded."** It is found in the first verse of our Torah reading.

## Deuteronomy 3:23-24

"I pleaded with Adonai at that time, saying, **24** 'O Lord Adonai, You have begun to show Your servant Your greatness and Your strong hand—for what god is there in heaven or on earth who can do deeds and mighty acts like Yours?"

## Scripture Readings:

Deuteronomy 3:23-7:11, Isaiah 40:1-26, Luke 3:2-15, Psalm 90

## The Theme of the Torah Portion:

Do and keep the commandments

## Scripture for Theme

## Deuteronomy 6:4

You must keep and do them, for it is your wisdom and understanding in the eyes of the peoples, who will hear all these statutes and say, 'Surely this great nation is a wise and understanding people.'

# Torah Portion Outline

- Moses Pleads to Enter the Promised Land, **Deuteronomy 3:23-29**
- Listen and Obey, **Deuteronomy 4:1-9**
- When Adonai Spoke From the Fiery Mountain, **Deuteronomy 4:11-49**
- The Ten Commandments, **Deuteronomy 5:1-19**
- Obey, Live, and Prolong Your Days, **Deuteronomy 5:20-29**
- Teaching the Commandments in the Land, **Deuteronomy 6:1-3**
- Shema Israel, **Deuteronomy 6:4-9**
- Do Not Forget Adonai When You prosper, **Deuteronomy 6:10-19**
- When Your Son Asks, **Deuteronomy 6:20-25**
- Do Not Mix with Idolaters, **Deuteronomy 7:1-11**

# LESSON SUMMARY

Moses pleaded with Adonai to allow him to see the promised land. Moses could not enter the land because he struck the rock when Adonai told him to speak to the rock to get water. Adonai was angry at Moses and told him no, stop asking. Adonai told him to go to the top of Mount Pisgah, lift his eyes toward the west, the north, the south, the east, and he would see all the land but he would not enter it. At that time, Adonai commanded Moses to anoint Joshua and appoint him as the new leader to lead the people into the promised land.

The children of Israel were still in the land of Moab east of the Jordan when Moses began to teach them all the commandments Adonai gave at Mount Sinai. He taught them the importance of listening, following, and obeying the commandments as they entered the land Adonai was giving them. He said to them; "You must not add to the word that I am commanding you or take away from it—in order to keep the mitzvot of Adonai your God that I am commanding you to" (Deuteronomy 4:2). He also warned them of what would happen to them if they forget to keep Adonai's commandments. He declared to them; "Your eyes have seen what Adonai did at Baal Peor, for Adonai your God has destroyed from among you everyone who followed Baal Peor. But you who held tight to Adonai your God are alive today—all of you" (Deuteronomy 4:3-4). Moses gave them the Ten Commandments that Adonai gave their fathers at Mount Sinai. They were instructed not to make any image to represent Adonai because when He spoke to them from the fire they did not see a form or an image. From this Torah portion, we learn what is known as the greatest commandment. It is known as "The Shema." "Hear O Israel, the Lord our God, the Lord is one. 5 Love Adonai your God with all your heart and with all your soul and with all your strength"(Deuteronomy 6:4-5).

Moses constantly emphasized that if they wanted to live and remain in the land and have a long life, they were to diligently follow Adonai and not to forget Him when they had settled in the land and when everything was going well for them. They were to teach His commandments to their children and grandchildren. He told them that in the future when they had settled in the land and their sons asked them, "Why do we keep all these commandments?," they were to tell them how they were slaves in Egypt, and how Adonai brought them out of Egypt with a mighty hand. They were to explain how Adonai showed signs and wonders to give them a land He swore to their fathers; and that keeping the commands is for their good. Deuteronomy 6:20-25.

The Torah reading ends with Moses reminding the children of Israel not to keep company, learn the ways, or marry any of the idol worshipers from the seven nations; the Hittites, the Girgashites, the Amorites, the Canaanites, the Perizzites, the Hivites, and the Jebusites whom Adonai was driving out the land He gave them to possess.

## LESSON DISCUSSION

### Listen and Live

Moses highlighted the importance of obedience to the commandments as a guide to how the children of Israel would survive and live in the land that Adonai gave to possess.

### Learning Points From this Torah Portion:
- Listen and live
- Fear Adonai and live
- Wisdom and understanding are found in the commandments
- Don't forget Adonai
- Teach the Commandments to your children and grandchildren
- Adonai is a jealous God
- Don't follow other gods
- Do what is right and good in Adonai's sight
- Adonai's anger is like fire, it destroys everything
- Do not make any image to represent Adonai and worship it
- Worship and serve Adonai only

### Adonai's Commandments are the Foundation of Life.
Everything God wants us to know and do is written in His Torah for us to follow.

### Deuteronomy 6:4-9
4 "Hear O Israel, the Lord our God, the Lord is one. 5 Love Adonai your God with all your heart and with all your soul and with all your strength. 6 These words, which I am commanding you today, are to be on your heart. 7 You are to teach them diligently to your children, and speak of them when you sit in your house, when you walk by the way, when you lie down and when you rise up. 8 Bind them as a sign on your hand, they are to be as frontlets between your eyes, 9 and write them on the doorposts of your house and on your gates.

Moses sets the foundation for the children of Israel as they go to possess the promised land. He reminded them that Adonai made a covenant with them at Mount Sinai when they heard His voice from the fire. Moses gave them the "BIG TEN" (Ten Commandments). The Ten Commandments are the foundation for every generation to learn to fear, obey, and serve Adonai.

- Ask the children if they remember what the Ten Commandments are, and to tell you the "BIG TEN." Exodus 20:1-19, Deuteronomy 5:1-19
- Ask why they think it was important for Moses to tell this second generation the "BIG TEN."
- Do you think it is important for you to know and keep them? Why?

**The Greatest Commandment**

Thousand of years after Adonai gave the Ten Commandments Yeshua was asked what is the greatest commandment in Torah.

**Matthew 22:35-40**

And testing Him, one of them, a lawyer, asked, **36** "Teacher, which is the greatest commandment in the Torah?" **37** And He said to him, "You shall love Adonai your God with all your heart, and with all your soul, and with all your mind.' **38** This is the first and greatest commandment. **39** And the second is like it, 'You shall love your neighbor as yourself.' **40** The entire Torah and the Prophets hang on these two commandments."

**Yeshua lived many generations after Adonai gave Moses the commandments on Mount Sinai, but they were still necessary to learn, obey, and follow in His generation.**

**As His disciples, we should follow His example.**

**John 15:9-12 The Message**
"I've loved you the way my Father has loved me. Make yourselves at home in my love. If you keep my commands, you'll remain intimately at home in my love. That's what I've done—kept my Father's commands and made myself at home in his love. "I've told you these things for a purpose: that my joy might be your joy, and your joy wholly mature. This is my command: Love one another the way I loved you."

## TURNING POINT:

## A LOVE AND A PROMISE:

From the time God made His promise to Abraham, He has been faithful. God told Abraham, "Leave your country, your family, and your father's home for a land that I will show you. I'll make you a great nation and bless you. I'll make you famous; you'll be a blessing. I'll bless those who bless you; those who curse you I'll curse. All the families of the Earth will be blessed through you."Genesis 12:1-3

Abraham loved Adonai and had a personal relationship with Him, the Eternal God. He trusted God and believed He would do exactly as He promised. In this week's Torah portion, Moses reminds the children of Israel, that God did not choose them because they were a great nation, but because of His love and the covenant promise He made to their ancestors: Abraham, Isaac, and Jacob. Moses said to them, "God wasn't attracted to you and didn't choose you because you were big and important—the fact is, there was almost nothing to you. He did it out of sheer love, keeping the promise he made to your ancestors. God stepped in and mightily bought you back out of that world of slavery, freed you from the iron grip of Pharaoh king of Egypt. Know this: God, your God, is God indeed, a God you can depend upon. He keeps his covenant of loyal love with those who love him and observe his commandments for a thousand generations. But he also pays back those who hate him, pays them the wages of death; he isn't slow to pay them off—those who hate him, he pays right on time. So keep the command and the rules and regulations that I command you today. Do them" **(Deuteronomy 7:7-11 MSG)**.

You are reading this today because your parents love and follow Adonai and they want you to also learn to love and follow Him. They might have learned about Adonai from their parents or a good friend, then they decided to have a personal relationship with Him. In their relationship with Him, they have learned He is faithful. If you ask your parents to tell you how God demonstrated his faithfulness in their lives, you will see that it is not because of anything great they have done, but because of His love and covenant promises.

The first generation of Israel who came out of Egypt that were twenty (20) years and older died in the wilderness because they did not trust Adonai and believed His words; except for Joshua and Caleb. Now Moses encouraged their children not to make the same mistakes as the first generation of Israel did. He warns them if they want to live, they should love, obey, and follow Adonai.

Like this generation that stood before Moses learning the commandments Adonai gave to their fathers and to trust Adonai's word to possess the land, you too will have to make a personal decision to choose to serve Adonai with all your heart and discover His faithfulness in your life, or forget Him.

**Do you believe Adonai's Words are true?**

## PRACTICAL APPLICATIONS

### FOR CHILDREN 4-6 YEARS OLD

Parents, please read Psalm 119:17-32 as a declaration over your child/children.

### FOR CHILDREN 7-12 YEARS OLD

Parents, please read Psalm 119:17-32 as a declaration over your child/children.

Children, please read four verses each night before bed from Psalm 119:17-32.

### FOLLOW-UP FROM THE LAST TORAH PORTION

Ask who wants to share from last week's practical application.

### FOR CHILDREN 4-6 YEARS OLD

Parents, please read Psalm 119:1-16 as a declaration over your child/children.

### FOR CHILDREN 7-12 YEARS OLD

Parents, please read Psalm 119:1-16 as a declaration over your child/children.

Children, please read three verses each night before bed from Psalm 119:1-16.

# QUESTIONS - TEACHERS ANSWER KEY

**1. What was Moses' plea to Adonai?**
To let him cross over the Jordan and enter the promised land

**2. Why were the children of Israel commanded not to make any image representing Adonai?**
They did not see an image or form when He spoke to them from the fire

**3. From which mountain did Moses see the promised land?**
Pisgah

**4. How many nations would Adonai drive out of the land for Israel to possess? Name three of them:**
Seven (7) nations: <u>Hittites</u>, <u>Girgashites</u>, <u>Amorites</u>, <u>Canaanites</u>, <u>Perizzites</u>, <u>Hivites</u>, and <u>Jebusites</u>

**5. According to Deuteronomy 4:2, what two things did Moses tell the children of Israel not to do?**
Do not add to or take away from the word he was teaching them

**6. What is the greatest commandment also known as?**
The Shema

**7. What is the second greatest commandment in the Torah according to Yeshua? (Matthew 22:39)**
Love your neighbor as yourself

**8. To whom were the children of Israel commanded to teach the commandments of Adonai?**
Their children and grandchildren

**9. To what is Adonai's anger compared?**
Consuming Fire

**10. According to Deuteronomy 6:7, when should parents teach their children the commandments of Adonai?**
When you sit in the house, walk on the road, when you lie down, and when you rise up

# QUESTIONS - CHILDREN'S COPY

1. What was Moses' plea to Adonai?

2. Why were the children of Israel commanded not to make any image representing Adonai?

3. From which mountain did Moses see the promised land?

4. How many nations would Adonai drive out the land for Israel to possess? _____ Name three of them: _____, _____, _____

5. According to Deuteronomy 4:2, what two things did Moses tell the children of Israel not to do?

6. What is the greatest commandment also known as?

7. What is the second greatest commandment in the Torah according to Yeshua? (Matthew 22:39)

8. To whom were the children of Israel commanded to teach the commandments of Adonai?

9. To what is Adonai's anger compared?

10. According to Deuteronomy 6:7, when should parents teach their children their children the commandments of Adonai?

## CRAFTS SUPPLIES FOR TORAH PORTION VA'ETCHANAN

**SUPPLIES:**
1. Foam Picture Frames With Stickers can be purchased on Amazon
2. Phone Camera
3. Printer
4. Paper
5. Stickers
6. Gems

## CRAFTS: SHEMA ISRAEL

1. Prep done by the teacher: Take pictures of each child with their eyes closed, as if they are reciting the Shema. In a Word document insert the picture, then type up the prayer next to it. Print it out.

2. Children will each receive their picture with prayer pre-cut.

3. They will also receive foam picture frames and foam stickers.

4. Place the picture inside the frame. Secure with sticky foam outer frame.

5. Have each child recite and memorize both Hebrew and English versions.

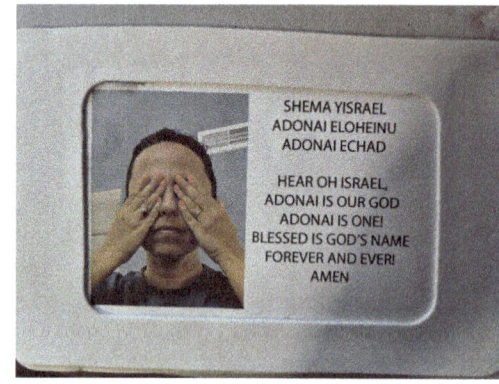

6. Decorate it with foam stickers and gems.

FINAL WORK

# Ekev

## "Because"

# Torah Portion 46: Ekev

The title of this week's Torah Portion is Ekev, which is translated as "**because or reward**." It is found in the first verse of our Torah reading.

### Deuteronomy 7:12 NASB
"Then it shall come about, **because** you listen to these judgments and keep and do them, that the Lord your God will keep with you His covenant and His lovingkindness which He swore to your forefathers.

### Deuteronomy 7:12 ArtScroll Translation
This shall be the **reward** when you hearken to these ordinances, and you observe and perform them; Hashem, your God, will safeguard for you the covenant and the kindness that He swore to your fathers.

## Scripture Readings:
Deuteronomy 7:12-11:25, Isaiah 49:14-51:3, Matthew 16:4-20, Psalm 75

**The Theme of the Torah Portion:**

A Heart of Obedience

**Scripture for Theme**

**Deuteronomy 10:16 CJB**

Therefore, circumcise the foreskin of your heart; don't be stiffnecked any longer!

# Torah Portion Outline

- A Covenant of Kindness, **Deuteronomy 7:12-17**
- The Assurance of Adonai's Protection, **Deuteronomy 7:18-26**
- Not By Bread Alone, **Deuteronomy 8:1-10**
- Warning Against Pride, **Deuteronomy 8:11-20**
- Remembering the Exodus, **Deuteronomy 9:1-12**
- Receiving the First Two Tablets, **Deuteronomy 9:13-21**
- Recalling Israel's Rebellions, **Deuteronomy 9:22-29**
- The Second Pair of Tablets, **Deuteronomy 10:1-11**
- What Adonai Requires, **Deuteronomy 10:12-22**
- Love and Obedience Rewarded, **Deuteronomy 11:1-25**

# LESSON SUMMARY

Last week's Torah Portion reading ended with Moses telling the children of Israel not to learn the ways, keep company with, or marry any of the idol worshipers from the seven nations whom Adonai was going to drive out the promised land He was giving them to possess. In this week's Torah Portion, Moses continues to instruct the children of Israel in the commandments of Adonai, encouraging them to obey and follow all that he is commanding them. He tells them of the rewards for obeying and the punishment they will endure if they disobey Adonai's commandments and His voice.

Moses spoke to them and said; these are the rewards that you will receive if you listen, keep, and do all Adonai's commandments because of the covenant of kindness that he established with their ancestors. "He will love you, bless you, and multiply you. He will also bless the fruit of your womb and the produce of your soil, your grain and your new wine and your oil, the increase of your herds and the young of your flock, in the land that He swore to your fathers to give you. From all peoples, you will be blessed—there will not be male or female barren among you or your livestock. Adonai will remove all sickness from you, and He will not inflict on you any of the terrible diseases of Egypt that you knew, but will inflict them on all who hate you." Deuteronomy 7:13-15 TLV

Moses assures them of Adonai's protection as they go to possess the land. He is the one going before them to drive out the other nations so they don't need to be afraid. He will cause great confusion among the nations to destroy them. Little by little He will drive out the nations, not all at once, so the beast of the field will not multiply and devour the children of Israel. Moses recounted to Israel all that Adonai had done for them in the wilderness; He clothed them and protected them from scorpions and fiery serpents. He fed them when they were hungry because He wanted to test them, to know what was in their hearts; if they would obey all His commandments or not. He gave them manna so they would understand that man must not live by bread alone but by all the words that Adonai speaks. Moses encouraged them to keep the commandments and fear Adonai, "For the Lord your God is bringing you into a good land, a land of brooks of water, of fountains and springs, flowing forth in valleys and hills; a land of wheat and barley, of vines and fig trees and pomegranates, a land of olive oil and honey; a land where you will eat food without scarcity, in which you will not lack anything; a land whose stones are iron, and out of whose hills you can dig copper. When you have eaten and are satisfied, you shall bless the Lord your God for the good land which He has given you." Deuteronomy 8:7-10 NIV

Moses told the children of Israel not to become prideful or boast about their righteousness when they possessed the land because it was not by their righteousness that Adonai chose them. He chose them because of the wickedness of the nations dwelling in the promised land and the covenant He had made with their forefathers: Abraham, Isaac, and Jacob. He warned them not to provoke Adonai and rebel like their fathers did when they made and worshiped the golden calf, or when they had murmured against Adonai. He also warned them not to be like Datan and Abiram who rebelled and were destroyed. Moses made known to them that Adonai would have destroyed them if he had not pleaded to Him on their behalf when they provoked Adonai to wrath with the golden calf. Moses was also angry with them and threw down the two tablets that Adonai gave him with the Ten Commandments (Ten Words) and broke them. After breaking them he was instructed to make two more tablets from stone, like the first pair, and an ark from wood; then to come back up to the mountain so Adonai could write on them as He did with the first two tablets. Forty days later Moses returned from the mountain with the new tablets and placed them in the ark which he made. He ordered the children of Israel not to forget Adonai when they entered the land for He would destroy them just like the nations He is droving out for them (Deuteronomy 8:19-20).

Moses' Advice to them was to love Adonai and keep His commandments, His statutes, and His ordinances at all times so they would be strong and go in and possess the promised land. If they did as Adonai commanded, Moses told them, every place where their feet walked would be theirs from the wilderness to Lebanon, from the Euphrates River to the Western Sea, that would be their border. No one would be able to face them and fight against them for Adonai would make the nations afraid of them.

# LESSON DISCUSSION

Moses in this Torah Portion continues to encourage the children of Israel to follow, obey, love, fear, and trust Adonai so they will possess, and live a long and prosperous life, in the land He was giving them. Moses told them of the rewards they would receive if they continued to obey all of Adonai's commands. He also told them of their fathers' rebellion in the wilderness and warned them not to make the same mistakes. He wanted them to understand that trusting Adonai and obeying Him was the best way to live a long and peaceful life. One of the things Moses encouraged the children of Israel to do was not to become like the other nations and worship idols.

Moses tells them the consequences if they disobey, "Watch yourselves, so your heart is not deceived, and you turn aside and serve other gods and worship them. Then the anger of Adonai will be kindled against you, so He will shut up the sky so that there will be no rain and the soil will not yield its produce. Then you will perish quickly from the good land Adonai is giving you." Deuteronomy 11:16-17

## THE REWARDS OF OBEDIENCE

### Deuteronomy 7:11-16 TLV
Then it will happen, as a result of your listening to these ordinances, when you keep and do them, that Adonai your God will keep with you the covenant kindness that He swore to your fathers.
- **He will love you**
- **He will bless you**
- **He will multiply you**
- **He will bless the fruit of your body**
- **He will bless the produce of your field**
- **He will bless your grain, your new wine, and your oil**
- **He will bless your herds and your flocks**
- **There will be no unfruitfulness**
- **He will remove all sickness from you**

Multiple times Moses advised and spoke about loving Adonai and obeying Him.

**How do we love and obey Adonai in our lives? Let's take a look at what our Torah Portion says.**

**LOVE AND OBEDIENCE ARE FROM THE HEART.**

**Deuteronomy 10:16 NASB**
"Circumcise the foreskin of your heart therefore, and do not be stiff-necked anymore.

**Deuteronomy 11: 13 The Voice**
If you carefully obey My commands which I'm giving you today, and if you love Me and serve Me with your whole heart and soul.

**Deuteronomy 11:18-21 The voice**
So let what I'm saying sink deeply into your hearts and souls. Do whatever it takes to remember what I'm telling you: tie a reminder on your hand or put a reminder on your forehead where you'll see it all the time, and on the doorpost where you cross the threshold or on the city gate. Teach these things to your children. Talk about them when you're sitting together in your home and when you're walking together down the road. Make them the last thing you talk about before you go to bed and the first thing you talk about the next morning. That way you and your children will be blessed with long life and abundant crops upon the ground the Eternal promised to your ancestors, for as long as there's a sky above the earth.

**To love and obey Adonai is a decision you make first in your heart then you are empowered to do what He said you are to do.**

**Adonai's rewards are endless for those who trust and obey Him. Only those who demonstrate their love for Him can benefit from His rewards.**

Adonai demonstrated (proved) His love for the children of Israel and brought them out of Egypt, the house of slavery. He provided for them, protected them, and gave them a fruitful land that they did not have to work for. He did it, not because they were righteous or perfect or because they were the greatest nation on earth, He did it because of the love He had for their forefathers and the covenant He had made with them.

**Adonai demonstrated the same love for us as well.**

When we did not deserve His love, because of sin, Adonai sent His Son, Yeshua to die for us and pay the price for our sins so we can have a relationship with Him. Romans 6:23 tells us that the punishment of sin is death, but the gift of God is eternal life through Yeshua.

**Romans 5:6-9**

When the time was right, the Anointed One died for all of us who were far from God, powerless, and weak. **7** Now it is rare to find someone willing to die for an upright person, although it's possible that someone may give up his life for one who is truly good. **8** But think about this: while we were wasting our lives in sin, God revealed His powerful love to us in a tangible display—the Anointed One died for us. **9** As a result, the blood of Jesus has made us right with God now, and certainly we will be rescued by Him from God's wrath in the future.

**What does Adonai require of us? The same response that He required of the children of Israel; listen, obey, and trust Him with all our hearts.**

**Deuteronomy 11:1**
Therefore you are to love Adonai your God and keep His charge, His statutes, His ordinances and His mitzvot at all times.

**1 John 2:1-6**
My children, I am writing these things to you so that you will not sin. But if anyone does sin, we have an Intercessor with the Father—the righteous Messiah Yeshua. **2** He is the atonement for our sins, and not only for our sins but also for the whole world.
**3** Now we know that we have come to know Him by this—if we keep His commandments. **4** The one who says, "I have come to know Him," and does not keep His commandments is a liar, and the truth is not in him. **5** But whoever keeps His word, in him the love of God is truly made perfect. We know that we are in Him by this—
**6** whoever claims to abide in Him must walk just as He walked.

**TURNING POINT:**

**Not By Bread Alone - Catching the Wind**

**Deuteronomy 8:1-3 The Message (MSG)**
Keep and live out the entire commandment that I'm commanding you today so that you'll live and prosper and enter and own the land that God promised to your ancestors. Remember every road that God led you on for those forty years in the wilderness, pushing you to your limits, testing you so that he would know what you were made of, whether you would keep his commandments or not. He put you through hard times. He made you go hungry. Then he fed you with manna, something neither you nor your parents knew anything about, so you would learn that men and women don't live by bread only; we live by every word that comes from God's mouth.

Moses told the children of Israel that Adonai fed them with Manna so they would learn that man does not live by bread alone, but by every word that comes from the mouth of God. Does this mean that we don't need to eat, or have houses, or clothes? Of course not. But Adonai wanted them to understand that everything they had or received in life, came from Him. King Solomon said, "This chasing after things is like trying to catch the wind" (Ecclesiastes 1:14).

Repeatedly in this Torah Portion, Moses tells the children of Israel about the blessings, or rewards, they will receive if they listen and obey Adonai's commands, and serve Him only. We too have the same promises if we learn to live by the words that come from the Mouth of Adonai (His commands) and not by living our lives trying to catch the wind (living according to our way).

Even Yeshua warned us about "trying to catch the wind." He said in Matthew chapter six, "If you decide for God, living a life of God-worship, it follows that you don't fuss about what's on the table at mealtimes or whether the clothes in your closet are in fashion. There is far more to your life than the food you put in your stomach, more to your outer appearance than the clothes you hang on your body. Look at the birds, free and unfettered, not tied down to a job description, careless in the care of God. And you count far more to him than birds (Mathew 6:25-26 MSG).

Don't waste your life trying to catch the wind. Seek Yeshua the Bread of Life and follow Adonai's commands.

**John 6:35 NIV**
Then Jesus declared, "I am the bread of life. Whoever comes to me will never go hungry, and whoever believes in me will never be thirsty.

When you are faced with making a choice, ask yourself: "Am I chasing the wind or words from Adonai?

## PRACTICAL APPLICATIONS

### FOR CHILDREN 4-6 YEARS OLD

Parents, please read Psalm 119:33-48 as a declaration over your child/children.

### FOR CHILDREN 7-12 YEARS OLD

Parents, please read Psalm 119:33-48 as a declaration over your child/children.

Children, please read three verses each night before bed from Psalm 119:33-48.

### FOLLOW-UP FROM THE LAST TORAH PORTION

Ask who wants to share from last week's practical application.

### FOR CHILDREN 4-6 YEARS OLD

Parents, please read Psalm 119:17-32 as a declaration over your child/children.

### FOR CHILDREN 7-12 YEARS OLD

Parents, please read Psalm 119:17-32 as a declaration over your child/children.

Children, please read three verses each night before bed from Psalm 119:17-32.

# QUESTIONS - TEACHERS ANSWER KEY

**1. What was the word used to describe the covenant? Deuteronomy 11:12**

Kindness

**2. What is the required behavior for receiving Adonai's reward?**

Listen, Keep, and do the commandments of Adonai

**3. With Whom did Adonai make His covenant?**

Abraham, Isaac, and Jacob

**4. Name some of the blessings/rewards for obedience. Deuteronomy 11**

He will love you, He will bless you, He will multiply you, He will bless the fruit of your body, He will bless the produce of your field, He will bless your grain, new wine, your oil, He will bless your herds and your flocks, There will be no unfruitfulness, He will remove all sickness from you

**5. Why did Adonai test the children of Israel?**

To know what was in their hearts, whether they would obey His commandments or not

**6. For what purpose did Adonai make the children of Israel experience hunger and feed them with Manna?**

So they would understand that man/woman does not eat by bread alone but by every word that comes from the mount of Adonai

**7. How many days and nights did Moses spend on the mountain each time he received the two tablets with the Ten Words?**

40 days and 40 nights

**8. Love and obedience come from the <u>heart.</u>**

**9. In what way did Adonai prove His love for the children of Israel? (Answer will vary depending on children's understanding)**

Adonai demonstrated (proved) His love for the children of Israel by bringing them out of Egypt, the house of slavery. He provided for them, protected them, and gave them a fruitful land that they did not have to work for.

**10. In what way did Adonai prove His love for us? (Answer will vary depending on children's understanding)**

When we did not deserve His love, because of sin, Adonai sent His Son, Yeshua to die for us and pay the price for our sins so we can have a relationship with Him.

## QUESTIONS - CHILDREN'S COPY

1. What was the word used to describe the covenant? Deuteronomy 11:12

2. What is the required behavior for receiving Adonai's reward?

3. With Whom did Adonai make His covenant?

4. Name some of the blessings/rewards for obedience. Deuteronomy 11

5. Why did Adonai test the children of Israel?

6. For what purpose did Adonai make the children of Israel hungry and feed them with Manna?

7. How many days and nights did Moses spend on the mountain each time he received the two tablets with the Ten Words?

8. Love and obedience come from the _____.

9. In what way did Adonai prove His love for the children of Israel?

10. In what way did Adonai prove His love for us?

# CRAFTS SUPPLIES FOR TORAH PORTION EKEV

**SUPPLIES:**
1. White Cardstock
2. Red Construction Paper
3. Black Construction Paper
4. Gems
5. Print Paper
6. Glue Sticks
7. Markers, Pencils, Crayons

# CRAFTS: CIRCUMCISED HEART

1. Glue red heart on white cardstock.
2. Match the white heart to the red heart so all the edges line up.
3. Put sticky tape on the notch of the red heart, then fold it to attach the white heart to it.

 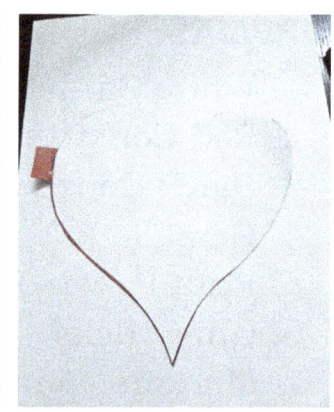

4. Glue black pieces of the heart as shown on top of the white heart, to represent a stony heart.
5. Glue black and red pieces on the inside of the white heart.

6. Decorate the red heart with gems.
7. Glue the header 'Circumcised Heart' as shown and color it.

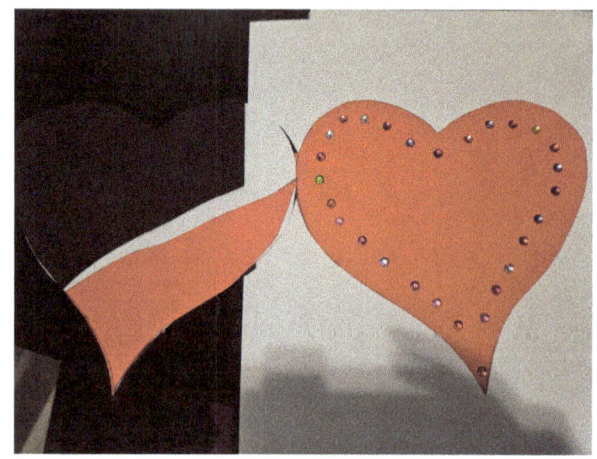

8. Glue Scripture verses on the inside of the stony heart.
9. Label the hearts.

FINAL WORK

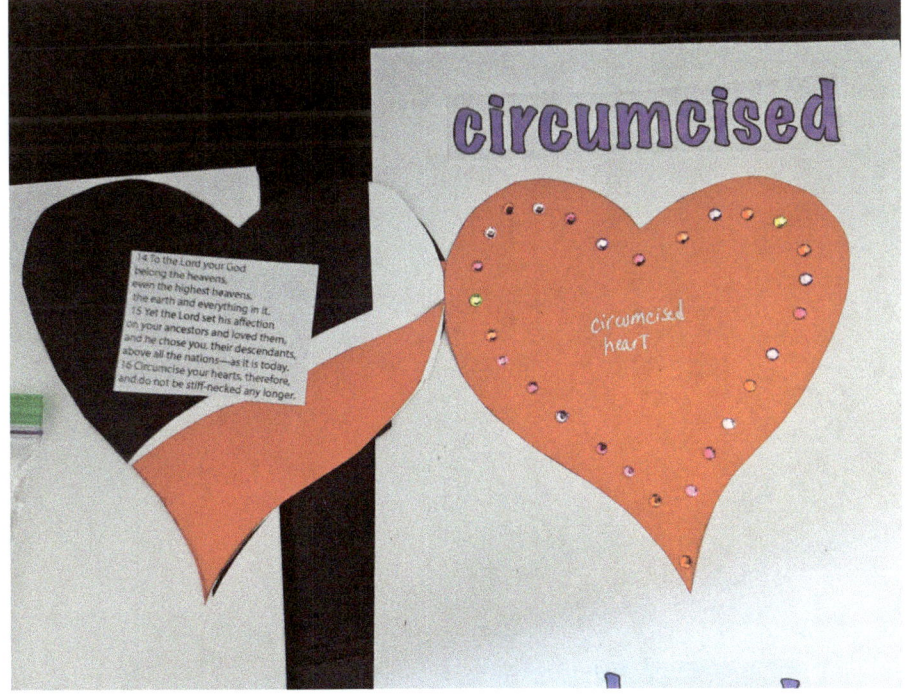

# Re'eh

## "See"

# Torah Portion 47: Re'eh

The title of this week's Torah Portion is **Re'eh**; it is translated as **"see"** in the first verse of our Torah reading.

## Deuteronomy 11:26 NASB

"**See**, I am setting before you today a blessing and a curse:"

## Scripture Readings:

Deuteronomy 11:26-16:17, Isaiah 54:11-55:5, John 6:35-51, Psalm 97

## The Theme of the Torah Portion:

The Place Adonai Chooses to Put His Name

## Scripture for Theme

## Deuteronomy 12:5

But you shall seek the Lord at the place which the Lord your God will choose from all your tribes, to establish His name there for His dwelling, and there you shall come.

# Torah Portion Outline

- Blessing and Curse, **Deuteronomy 11:26-32**
- A Prescribed Place of Worship, **Deuteronomy 12:1-8**
- Private Altars, **Deuteronomy 12:9-14**
- Regulations for Redeemed Offerings, Foods Offered Only in Jerusalem, and Unconsecrated Meets, **Deuteronomy 12:15-28**
- Beware of False Gods, **Deuteronomy 12:29-32**
- A False Prophet, **Deuteronomy 13:1-6**
- One Who Entices You to Go Astray, **Deuteronomy 13:7-12**
- A City of Lawlessness, **Deuteronomy 13:13-19**
- Adonai's Treasure, **Deuteronomy 14:1-2**
- Permitted and Forbidden Foods,
- **Deuteronomy 14:3-21**
- Principles of Tithing, **Deuteronomy 3:22-29**
- Debts Canceled Every Seven Years, **Deuteronomy 15:1-6**
- Giving to the Poor, **Deuteronomy 15:7-11**
- Laws for Bondservants, **Deuteronomy 15:12-18**
- Laws for Firstborn Animals, **Deuteronomy 15: 19-23**
- Review of the Feast Days, **Deuteronomy 16:1-17**

# LESSON SUMMARY

Last week's Torah portion ended with Moses telling the children of Israel that if they did as Adonai commanded, every place where their foot walked would be theirs from the wilderness to Lebanon, from the Euphrates River to the Western Sea, would be their border; no nation would be able to face them in battle because Adonai would fight for them. God's assurance to His people is that if they obey, they will be rewarded.

In this Torah Portion, Re'eh, Moses said to the children of Israel, "See I am setting before you today a blessing and a curse." They will receive a blessing if they listen to Adonai's commands, or a curse if they go after other gods. The blessings are to be set on Mount Gerizim and the curses on Mount Ebal when they have crossed over to possess the promised land.

Moses proclaimed the rules and laws of the land for the children of Israel. He said they were to utterly destroy all the places where the nations serve their gods. Do not act like these nations toward Adonai. Worship Him only in the place where Adonai chooses to put His Name to dwell among the tribes. Moses reminded them not to eat the blood of any animal so it would go well with them and their children. They were to be careful not to neglect the Levites either. The Holy things and vow offerings were to be taken to the place that Adonai chooses. Only animals that were not a part of the sacrifices and offerings for Adonai could be eaten in their towns as their hearts desired.

Moses instructed the children of Israel again saying, "Whatever I command you, you must take care to do, you are not to add or take away from it." Moses told them to beware of a false prophet or a dreamer from among them who gives a sign or wonder that comes true and then tries to influence them to follow other gods. Moses said don't listen to them because God is testing you to know whether you love Him with all your heart and with all your soul. The prophet and the dreamer must be put to death for speaking falsely against Adonai. He also warns, if anyone, whether a son, a brother, daughter, husband, or best friend tries to mislead you secretly to follow after other gods, you should not protect him. The person should be to death because he/she tries to entice you away from Adonai your God who brought you out of Egypt. When you hear that the people living in a city have become lawless and desire to go after and serve other gods, you should investigate to see if it is true. If it is true, you are to strike down the inhabitants of the city with the sword destroying it and all the livestock. Take nothing from the city to keep so that the fierce anger of Adonai may turn from you, show you mercy, have compassion on you, and multiply you just as He had promised your forefathers.

Moses also spoke to the children of Israel saying; "You are the children of ADONAI your God. You are not to cut yourselves or shave your forehead for the dead. For you are a holy people to ADONAI your God—from all the peoples on the face of the earth, ADONAI has chosen you to be His treasured people (Deuteronomy 14:1-2). He reminded them of Adonai's commands to eat only foods that Adonai described as clean and not to eat those He described as unclean. They were also commanded to set aside a tenth of the produce that grew in the field each year. They were commanded to bring a tithe also from the grain, wine, oil, and the firstborn from the herds and flock, and eat in the presence of Adonai in the place He designated. Moses continued, if the place Adonai chooses is too far from you to carry your tithe, you are to exchange (sell) your tithe for money and take the money to the palace chosen for worship Adonai; using the money to buy food that is good for you and your family, to feast in the presence of God, and have a good time.

The children of Israel were also commanded not to forget to take care of the Levites in their towns. At the end of every third year, they were to gather the tithe from all the produce of the year and put it aside in storage to keep in reserve for the Levites who had no property for their inheritance. The collected tithe would also serve the foreigner, the orphan, and the widow who lived among them, so they would have plenty to eat and Adonai would bless them. Every seven years creditors should cancel every debt. Every bondservant must be let free after six years of working, but he must not be let go empty handed; they were to give to them as Adonai has blessed them.

Moses declares, "If only you would carefully listen to the voice of Adonai your God, being careful to do all these mitzvah that I am commanding you today! For Adonai, your God will bless you as He promised you. So you will lend to many nations, but not borrow; you will rule over many nations, but they will not rule over you." (Deuteronomy 15:5-6). Don't be hardhearted toward the poor, lend to them freely whatever they need. Give generously to them, for this Adonai will bless you in all your work.

This Torah Portion ends with the ordinances for the observance of Passover, Shavuot, and Sukkot. These are the three festivals in which Adonai commands that men must appear before Him in the place He chooses and bring a gift because of the blessing Adonai has given.

## LESSON DISCUSSION

### THE PLACE - ADONAI'S DWELLING

In this Torah Portion, Moses said to the children of Israel, "See I have set before you today a blessing and a curse." A blessing if they listen and obey, and a curse if they did not listen to the voice of Adonai or obey His commands (Deuteronomy 11:26-31). He then proclaimed to them the laws and the rules of Adonai for how they should live in the land. Repeatedly Moses tells them to go to the place where Adonai chooses to put His Name. Even if the place is too far for them to bring the tithe from the produce of the land, they are to sell the produce and go to the place where Adonai chooses, and buy food to offer as a tithe unto Adonai. Only animals that were not a part of the sacrifices and offerings for Adonai could be eaten in their towns as their hearts desired. They were reminded not to act like the nations of the land they were to possess.

**The choices they made were important. It would determine whether they would receive a blessing or a curse.**

**In the Place Adonai Chooses:**
- Worship Him
- Bring your burnt offerings and sacrifices
- Tithes
- Offerings from your hands
- Vows and free will offerings
- Tithes from the firstborn of herds and flocks
- Rejoice before Adonai with your family, servants, and Levites

**Do you know what is the name of the Place Adonai chose to put His Name?** If children have their Bible, let them look up 1 Kings 11:36.

**1 Kings 11:36** — And his son I shall give one tribe so that David My servant may have a kingdom before Me in Jerusalem, the city which I chose for Myself to place My name there.

**We too have to choose to obey and listen to Adonai's commands. If we obey and listen to the voice of Adonai our God, we will receive the blessings, but if we don't obey Him, we will receive the curses.**

**John 15:7-11 TLV**
"If you abide in Me and My words abide in you, ask whatever you wish, and it shall be done for you. **8** In this My Father is glorified, that you bear much fruit and so prove to be My disciples." **9** "Just as the Father has loved Me, I also have loved you. Abide in My love! **10** If you keep My commandments, you will abide in My love, just as I have kept My Father's commandments and abide in His love. **11** These things I have spoken to you so that My joy may be in you, and your joy may be full.

**Romans 6:16**
Do you not know that to whatever you yield yourselves as slaves for obedience, you are slaves to what you obey—whether to sin resulting in death, or to obedience resulting in righteousness?

**The children of Israel were commanded to go to the place Adonai chose. Eat only clean animals, and don't consume the blood of animals. Nor were they to make any markings on their bodies for the dead because they are God's chosen treasure.**

**Our body is Adonai's dwelling place. We must be careful where we go, what we eat, and what we do to it.**

**2 Corinthians 6:14-18 New Living Translation (NLT)**

Don't team up with those who are unbelievers. How can righteousness be a partner with wickedness? How can light live with darkness?

**15** What harmony can there be between Christ and the devil? How can a believer be a partner with an unbeliever? **16** And what union can there be between God's temple and idols? For we are the temple of the living God. As God said: "I will live in them and walk among them. I will be their God, and they will be my people. **17** Therefore, come out from among unbelievers, and separate yourselves from them, says the Lord. Don't touch their filthy things, and I will welcome you. **18** And I will be your Father, and you will be my sons and daughters, says the Lord Almighty."

**Are you making the right choices?**

# TURNING POINT:

## Who Has Your Ears?

### Deuteronomy 13:5

Adonai your God you will follow and Him you will fear. His mitzvot you will keep, to His voice you will listen, Him you will serve and to Him you will cling.

In This week's Torah Portion, Moses warns the children of Israel about listening to a false prophet or a dreamer and protecting a city that has turned away from Adonai. Moses cautions them not to listen to the dreamer or prophet; even if what they said becomes true, because Adonai is testing them to know whether they will love Him with all their heart and all their soul. Moses tells them even if it is their brother, sister, or best friend who secretly tempts them to follow after other gods, they should not listen. Even if they hear that all the city people decide to turn away from following Adonai, the children of Israel are warned not to keep it a secret. They were to investigate and see if it was true or not. If it is true, those living in the city were to be punished for their sins, and the city destroyed.

What lesson(s) can we learn from this warning to follow and listen to Adonai only? In the Torah portion Va'etchanan, we learned that Adonai is a consuming (devouring) fire, and a jealous God (Deuteronomy 4:24). Following after other gods break the covenant Adonai made with His people. Breaking Adonai's covenant brings upon the person Adonai's anger. God doesn't have any favorites when it comes to punishing sin. He punished Israel for their sin, and He will also punish you for your sin.

Whenever anyone temps you to do something you know is against Adonai's commands, even if you are the only one, choose to do the right thing. Adonai will reward your obedience.

## PRACTICAL APPLICATIONS

### FOR CHILDREN 4-6 YEARS OLD

Parents, please read Psalm 119:49-64 as a declaration over your child/children.

### FOR CHILDREN 7-12 YEARS OLD

Parents, please read Psalm 119:49-64 as a declaration over your child/children.

Children, please read two verses each night before bed from Psalm 119:49-64.

### FOLLOW-UP FROM THE LAST TORAH PORTION

Ask who wants to share from last week's practical application.

### FOR CHILDREN 4-6 YEARS OLD

Parents, please read Psalm 119:33-48 as a declaration over your child/children.

### FOR CHILDREN 7-12 YEARS OLD

Parents, please read Psalm 119:33-48 as a declaration over your child/children.

Children, please read two verses each night before bed from Psalm 119:33-48.

# QUESTIONS - TEACHERS ANSWER KEY

1. **On which two mountains was the blessing and curse set for the children of Israel to see?** Blessing on Mount Gerizim and the curse on Mount Ebal

2. **Where was the only place that the children of Israel were allowed to worship?** The Place Adonai chooses to put His Name

3. Moses told the children of Israel not to neglect the **Levites** and the **stranger.**

4. **What must the children of Israel do with the places of worship of the other nations?** Destroy them completely

5. **What was to be done if the place Adonai chose to put His Name for worship was too far for the children of Israel to bring their tithe of the produce?** Sell the produce for tithe and go to the place Adonai chooses and buy food that is good, present it to Adonai, and worship Him

6. **What is the warning given about a prophet and a dreamer if they want you to serve other gods?**
Don't listen to them. Adonai is testing you

7. **According to 1 Kings 11:36, which city did Adonai choose to put His Name many years after the children of Israel possessed the land?** Jerusalem

8. **What kind of animals are considered clean?**
Animals that have split hooves and chew their cuds.

9. **What kind of sea creatures are considered clean?**
Fish that have fins and scales

10. **Other than unclean animals, what else were the children of Israel commanded not to eat?** Don't consume the blood of Animals

# QUESTIONS - CHILDREN'S COPY

1. On which two mountains was the blessing and curse set for the children of Israel to see?

2. Where was the only place that the children of Israel were allowed to worship?

3. Moses told the children of Israel not to neglect the _____ and the _____

4. What must the children of Israel do with the places of worship of the other nations?

5. What should be done if the place Adonai chose to put His Name for worship is too far for the children of Israel to bring their tithe of the produce?

6. What is the warning given about a prophet and a dreamer if they want you to serve other gods?

7. According to 1 Kings 11:36, which city did Adonai choose to put His Name many years after the children of Israel possessed the land?

8. What kind of animals are considered clean?

9. What kind of sea creatures are considered clean?

10. Other than unclean animals, what else were the children of Israel commanded not to eat?

# CRAFTS SUPPLIES FOR TORAH PORTION RE'EH

## SUPPLIES:
1. "12×12" Cardstock
2. Print Paper
3. Glue Stick
4. Pencils
5. Markers, Crayons
6. Crossword Puzzle Created Using www.education.com (Free tool)

# CRAFTS: CLEAN/UNCLEAN ANIMALS CROSSWORD

1. Children will glue a blank crossword puzzle in the middle of the cardstock.
2. They will glue cut-outs of animals/birds etc... These animals are their puzzle key, as most of these animals are in the crossword.

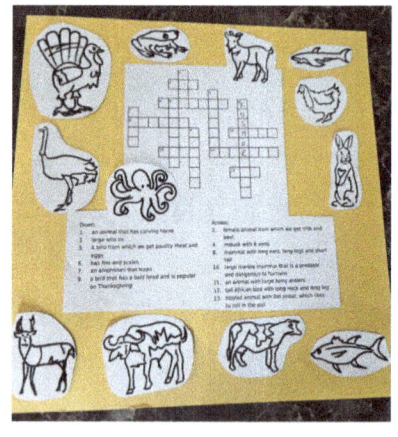

3. With the help of a teacher, children will complete the puzzle. *(The younger group will need a lot more help. Teachers, please walk around the classroom and help the children).*

4. With a highlighter, highlight CLEAN animals on the puzzle.
5. If time allows it, lightly color the animals.

THE COMPLETED PUZZLE

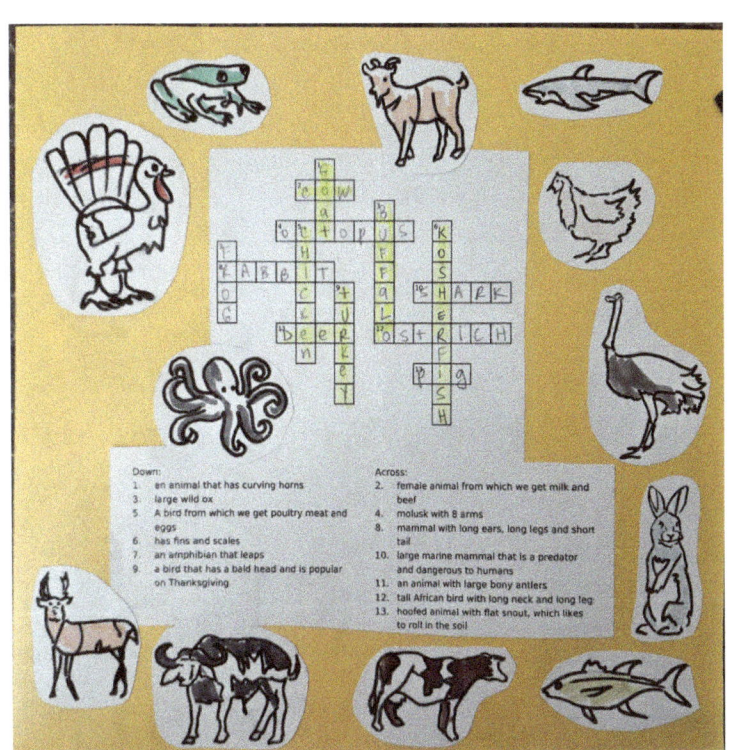

Page 70

# Shoftim
"Judges"

# Torah Portion 48: Shoftim

The Title of this week's Torah Portion is **"Shoftim"**. It is the Hebrew word translated as **"Judges"** in the first verse of our Torah reading.

### Deuteronomy 16:18 TLV
"**Judges** and officers you are to appoint within all your gates that Adonai your God is giving you, according to your tribes; and they are to judge the people with righteous judgment.

### Scripture Readings:
Deuteronomy 16:18-21:9, Isaiah 51:12-52:12, John 6:35, Psalm 17

## The Theme of the Torah Portion:

Pursue Righteousness

## Scripture for Theme

### Deuteronomy 16:20 Common English Bible (CEB)

"Righteousness! Pursue righteousness so that you live long and take possession of the land that the LORD your God is giving you."

# Torah Portion Outline

- Establishment of Judges, **Deuteronomy 16:18-20**

- No Idolatrous Trees or Blemished Sacrifice, **Deuteronomy 16:21-22**

- Penalty for Idol Worship, **Deuteronomy 17:1-13**

- Rules for a King, **Deuteronomy 17:14-20**

- Gifts for the Priests and Levites, **Deuteronomy 18:1-8**

- Pagan Worship Practices Forbidden, **Deuteronomy 18:9-14**

- A Prophet Like Moses, **Deuteronomy 18:15-22**

- Cities of Refuge, **Deuteronomy 19:1-13**

- Protecting the Land Boundaries, **Deuteronomy 19:14**

- Laws for Witnesses, **Deuteronomy 19:15-21**

- Principles for When Israel Goes to War, **Deuteronomy 20:1-20**

- Making Atonement for Unsolved Crimes, **Deuteronomy 21:1-9**

# LESSON SUMMARY

Moses told the children of Israel to appoint judges and officers in every town that the Lord was giving them. The judges were to judge in righteousness. They were not to show favoritism, nor accept bribes because a bribe would blind the eyes of the wise and would cause them to twist the truth. They were to seek justice at all times. They were not to set up any wooden Asherah poles next to the altar of Adonai, or a sacred pillar, because God hates idol worship. If anyone was suspected and accused of doing evil in the sight of Adonai by serving other gods or worshiping the sun, moon, or stars, the accusation was to be investigated. If the accusation was found to be true, the man or woman was to be put to death. Only by the evidence of two or three witnesses could an accusation be judged. Moses prophesied that the time would come when Israel would desire to be like the other nations and would want a king to rule them; the king was to be chosen from among the people. The king was to write the Torah for Himself in the presence of the Priest and the Levites and keep it at all times, read it, and learn to fear Adonai all the days of his life.

Moses instructed the people that the priests and the Levites were to receive gifts from the offerings made by fire unto Adonai. It was their inheritance among their brothers as Adonai had promised them. The Priest and Levites were to receive a portion of the offerings presented to Adonai as their Inheritance. They were to receive a share of the people's sacrifice, whether it was from a sheep or bull. They were to receive the first fruit from the grain, new wine, oil, and the first wool sheared from the flock. Moses also warned the people about practicing witchcraft, divination, consulting mediums, fortune tellers, one who casts spells, a spiritist, or anyone who calls up the dead. These practices are offensive to Adonai and are not allowed. Moses prophesied that Adonai would raise up a Prophet like himself from among them in the future. They should listen to him.

Moses instructed the people to build cities of refuge for anyone who accidentally killed his brother while they were in the field. He gave them the guidelines for protecting the innocent. They were told not to move their neighbors' land boundaries that their ancestors were to set in the land Adonai would give them.

He gave them rules for when they go out to war. Moses instructed them saying, "When you are approaching the battle, the priest shall come near and speak to the people. He shall say to them, 'Hear, O Israel, you are approaching the battle against your enemies today. Do not be fainthearted. Do not be afraid, or panic, or tremble before them, for the LORD your God is the one who goes with you, to fight for you against your enemies, to save you" (Deuteronomy 20:2-5). The officers were to speak to the people saying that if a man has planted a vineyard and hasn't eaten from it, is engaged to a woman, or is afraid, he should be exempt from going to war so they wouldn't discourage the hearts of the people. Commanders of the armies were to be appointed when the officers finished speaking to the people. Moses commanded the children of Israel not to cut down any fruit trees when they went to war against a city to make barricades. This Torah Portion ends with the rules and guidelines for when a person is found dead on the road and no one knows who killed that person.

## LESSON DISCUSSION

### Righteous Judgment

**Deuteronomy 16:18-20 TLV**
"Judges and officers you are to appoint within all your gates that Adonai your God is giving you, according to your tribes; and they are to judge the people with righteous judgment. **19** You are not to twist justice—you must not show partiality or take a bribe, for a bribe blinds the eyes of the wise and distorts the words of the righteous. **20** Justice, justice you must pursue, so that you may live and possess the land that Adonai your God is giving you. **21** You are not to plant for yourself an Asherah pole of any kind of wood beside the altar of Adonai your God that you make for yourself. **22** Nor are you to set up a pillar for yourself—Adonai your God hates this."

Moses commanded the people to appoint judges and officers in every town they lived in when they settled in the land.

**What does it mean to be righteous?**
A righteous person is someone who desires to please God and does what is right in God's eyes.

**These judges and officers had to judge the people and every situation according to Adonai's standard, not their own.**

**Judge with Righteous judgment**

- Do not twist justice (the truth and God's laws)
- Do not show favoritism (treat everyone with honesty)
- Do not take a bribe (payment of any kind from an accused person or a person accusing someone else). A bribe blinds the eyes of the wise (pretend not to know the truth) and distorts (misrepresent) the words of the righteous

- Pursue only justice, so that you may live and possess the land that Adonai your God is giving you

**The judges and officers were to judge by Adonai's standards, His commandments, and laws for righteousness.**

Moses told the children of Israel in this Torah Portion that Adonai would raise up a prophet like him from among them (Deuteronomy 18:15-22). In the Book Isaiah, the prophet Isaiah also spoke about Yeshua (the prophet like Moses), Isaiah declared that Yeshua will have the Spirit of Adonai resting on Him. He will not judge by what He sees but in righteousness.

**Isaiah 11:1-5 TLV**
"Then a shoot will come forth out of the stem of Jesse, and a branch will bear fruit out of His roots. **2** The Ruach of Adonai will rest upon Him, the Spirit of wisdom and insight, the Spirit of counsel and might, the Spirit of knowledge and of the fear of Adonai. **3** His delight will be in the fear of Adonai. He will not judge by what His eyes see, nor decide by what His ears hear. **4** But with righteousness He will judge the poor, and decide with fairness for the poor of the land. He will strike the land with the rod of His mouth, and with the breath of His lips He will slay the wicked. **5** Also righteousness will be the belt around His loins, and faithfulness the belt around His waist.

**Yeshua bears the fruit of righteousness by the Ruach (Spirit of Adonai). We too are commanded to bear fruit of righteousness by the Spirit of Adonai.**

Yeshua is our example to follow. He lived and demonstrated the righteousness of Adonai by the Spirit of Adonai. We need the Spirit of Adonai to teach us to judge right in everything we do.

**Galatians 5:22-23 TLV**

"But the fruit of the Ruach is love, joy, peace, patience, kindness, goodness, faithfulness, **23** gentleness, and self-control—against such things there is no law."

When we demonstrate the fruit of the Spirit (Ruach) we judge by the righteousness of God and live according to His commandments.

**How can you demonstrate righteousness towards your family and friends?**

**TURNING POINT:**

**Imitating the Potter, Not Harry**

Do you have a favorite cartoon, TV show, or movie you love to watch? Do you ever try to imitate or copy your favorite character? What kind of behavior does this character portray?

Throughout the Book of Devarim, Moses warns the children of Israel not to be like the nations Adonai is driving out of the land He is giving them. In this week's Torah portion, he warns them not to imitate the practices of these nations which are detestable (offensive) to Adonai. Whoever does these things will also become detestable to Adonai.

**Deuteronomy 18:9-14**
"When you enter the land which the LORD your God gives you, you shall not learn to imitate the detestable things of those nations.
**10** There shall not be found among you anyone who makes his son or his daughter pass through the fire, one who uses divination, one who practices witchcraft, or one who interprets omens, or a sorcerer,
**11** or one who casts a spell, or a medium, or a spiritist, or one who calls up the dead. **12** For whoever does these things is detestable to the LORD; and because of these detestable things the LORD your God will drive them out before you. **13** You shall be blameless before the LORD your God. **14** For those nations, which you shall dispossess, listen to those who practice witchcraft and to diviners, but as for you, the LORD your God has not allowed you *to do.*

In everything you do, your aim should be to please Adonai. As children, we learn to do many things by imitating the people around us. Even our faith is something we learn from others. The Apostle Paul told the Corinthian believers "Be imitators of me, just as I also am of Messiah" 1 Corinthians 11:1. Imitating others is not a bad thing as long as it does not cause you to follow practices that do not align with the principles of Torah. Be careful not to imitate others whose way of life is not pleasing to Adonai. Paul also told the believers in Ephesus, "Be imitators of God, as dearly loved children" Ephesians 5:1.

**Who are you imitating?**

## PRACTICAL APPLICATIONS

### FOR CHILDREN 4-6 YEARS OLD

Parents, please read Psalm 119:65-80 as a declaration over your child/children.

### FOR CHILDREN 7-12 YEARS OLD

Parents, please read Psalm 119:65-80 as a declaration over your child/children.

Children, please read three verses each night before bed from Psalm 119:65-80.

### FOLLOW-UP FROM THE LAST TORAH PORTION

Ask who wants to share from last week's practical application.

### FOR CHILDREN 4-6 YEARS OLD

Parents, please read Psalm 119:49-64 as a declaration over your child/children.

### FOR CHILDREN 7-12 YEARS OLD

Parents, please read Psalm 119:49-64 as a declaration over your child/children.

Children, please read three verses each night before bed from Psalm 119:49-64.

# QUESTIONS - TEACHERS ANSWER KEY

1. **Give two reasons a judge should not take a bribe. Deut. 16:19**
   It blinds the eyes of the wise and causes him to twist the truth

2. **What should a judge pursue/seek at all times?**
   Justice

3. **How many witnesses are needed for a case to be judged?**
   Two Witnesses

4. **What was the King commanded to write for himself?**
   A copy of the Torah

5. **What are some of the practices that are offensive to Adonai? Deut. 18:9-14**
   Divination, witchcraft, calling up the dead, consulting mediums and sorcerers, casting spells

6. **The children of Israel were commanded not to move their neighbor's land boundaries.**

7. **What kind of tree is not allowed to be cut down during war?**
   Fruit trees

8. **According to Deuteronomy 20:8, why should a man who is afraid not go to war?**
   So he would not cause the hearts of his brothers to be discouraged

9. **Who should be appointed in every city?**
   Judges and officers

10. **Moses said Adonai would raise up a prophet like him (Moses).**

## QUESTIONS - CHILDREN'S COPY

1. Give two reasons a judge should not take a bribe. Deut. 16:19

2. What should a judge pursue/seek at all times?

3. How many witnesses are needed for a case to be judged?

4. What was the King commanded to write for himself?

5. What are some of the practices that are offensive to Adonai?

6. The children of Israel were commanded not to move _____.

7. What kind of tree is not allowed to be cut down during war?

8. According to Deuteronomy 20:8, why should a man who is afraid not go to war?

9. Who should be appointed in every city?

10. Moses said Adonia will raise up a _____ like him (Moses).

## CRAFTS SUPPLIES FOR TORAH PORTION SHOFTIM

**SUPPLIES:**
1. "12x12" Cardstock
2. Finger Paints.
3. Brown/Beige Markers, Pencils, or Crayons
4. Fruit of the Spirit Stickers
5. Color Pencils
6. Paper Plates

# CRAFTS: FRUIT TREE

1. On a paper plate, put some green finger paint and dip your whole hand into the paint as shown.
2. On 12×12 cardstock with the pre-drawn tree trunk, put your hand on the paper in 4-5 spots as shown, to paint the leaves.

3. On the second paper plate, put 3-4 various colors as shown.
4. Ask the children to dip their fingertips into the paint, and then mark on the paper as shown to represent the fruit.

5. Color inside tree trunk and branches.
6. On each side of the tree trunk, please stick the fruit of the Spirit stickers and write down what they are next to them.

FINAL WORK

# Ki Tetze

## "When You Go Out"

## Torah Portion 49: Ki Tetze

The title of this week's Torah Portion is **Ki Tetze,** which is the Hebrew word translated as **"when you go out."** It is found in the first verse of our Torah reading.

### Deuteronomy 21:10 TLV

"When you go out to war against your enemies, and Adonai your God hands them over to you and you take them captive,

### Scripture Readings:

Deuteronomy 21:10-25:19, Isaiah 54:1-10, Matthew 24:29-42, Psalm 32

# The Theme of the Torah Portion:

Purity in the Land

## Scripture for Theme

### Deuteronomy 23:15 NASB

Since the Lord your God walks in the midst of your camp to deliver you and to defeat your enemies before you, therefore your camp must be holy; and He must not see anything indecent among you or He will turn away from you.

# Torah Portion Outline

- Women of Beauty, **Deuteronomy 21:10-14**
- Rights of the Firstborn, **Deuteronomy 21:15-17**
- The Rebellious Son, **Deuteronomy 21:18-21**
- Concern for Your Neighbor's Property, **Deuteronomy 22:1-4**
- Male and Female Clothing, **Deuteronomy 22:5**
- The Mother Bird, **Deuteronomy 22:6-7**
- Protective Fence, **Deuteronomy 22:8-10**
- Tzitzi, **Deuteronomy 22:11-12**
- Laws Regarding Marriage Relations, **Deuteronomy 22:13-21**
- Laws Concerning Adultery, **Deuteronomy 22:22-30**
- Those Forbidden to Enter the Congregation of Adonai, **Deuteronomy 23:1-8**
- Cleanness in the Camp, **Deuteronomy 23:9-14**
- Various Laws, **Deuteronomy 23:15-25**
- Laws Concerning Marriage & Divorce, **Deuteronomy 24:1-4**
- How to Treat Each Other, **Deuteronomy 24:5-22**
- Punishing the Guilty, **Deuteronomy 25:1-4**
- Levirate Marriage (The Duty of a Brother), **Deuteronomy 25:5-10**

- Treating Others with Dignity, **Deuteronomy 25:11-16**
- Remembering Amelek, **Deuteronomy 25:17-19**

# LESSON SUMMARY

This week's Torah Portion begins with Adonai's command for when the children of Israel go out to war against their enemies and take their enemies captive. Moses described a variety of Adonai laws from family relationships to how one should treat a bird.

Moses addressed the desire of a man when he sees a beautiful woman he takes captive during a war and wants to take her as his wife. Before he can take her as his wife, the woman must shave her head, trim her nails, change her clothes, sit in the house, and weep for her father and mother for a full month. The right of a firstborn is made clear if a man has two wives. If he loves one wife and hates the other and they both give him a son; he cannot give the inheritance of the firstborn to the son of the wife he loves if the older son is from the wife he hates. The inheritance of the firstborn belongs to the son of the hated wife because he is the firstborn son. He must acknowledge his son by giving him a double portion of all that he has.

Moses told the people the rules for a wayward and rebellious son. He said a man guilty of sin is sentenced to death and hung on a tree. He must be buried the same day, for cursed is a man who hangs on a tree. Do not pollute the land of Adonai. Anything that belongs to a brother (neighbor) that is lost or goes astray whether it is an ox, sheep, donkey, or his clothes must be brought back to him if he lives near. If he lives far away it must be kept until he comes searching for it. A mother bird is to be sent away before taking her eggs or young ones. A man should not wear clothes made for a woman, and a woman is not to wear clothes made for a man because it is detestable to Adonai. A guard rail must be set up around the roof when building a new house, to prevent the guilt of innocent blood on the house owner if someone falls off it. The laws forbidding mixture are discussed. Do not wear clothes made of linen and wool. Do not plant two kinds of seed in a vineyard, and do not plow a field with an ox and donkey tied together. Adonai also gave laws and punishment for a man who falsely accuses his wife of shameful behavior.

In this Torah Portion, we also see a reminder of the laws given in previous Torah Portions; such as making tzitzit, laws concerning marriage relations, and adultery. They were also reminded that Adonai forbids ancestral relationships, those who were not allowed to enter the congregation of Adonai, and anyone born of forbidden relationships to the tenth generation. The Ammonites and Moabites are forbidden to enter because they attacked the tired and weak as the children of Israel came out of Egypt and Balak hired Balaam to curse Israel in the wilderness.

Moses warned the children of Israel not to fight against the Edomites, for they were brothers, descendants of Esau. Neither were they to fight against Egypt because they lived as foreigners in the Land. He also warned them to keep the camp clean and holy at all times because Adoani walked among them and He should not see anything indecent and turn away from them. No unclean person should enter the camp either.

Moses described various other laws as well. Laws about how to treat a runaway slave, rules concerning loans and interest to a brother and a foreigner, making vows to Adonai, and marriage and divorce laws. Regulations regarding a stranger, an orphan, and a widow. A man newly married should not go to war. He should remain home for one year with his wife. He also gave them laws concerning kidnapping, and a Levirate marriage (the practice of a brother marrying his brother's wife after he dies to preserve the name and inheritance of the dead brother). Lending to the poor, and having just and honest measures for measuring weights. The Torah Portion ends with the command to remember Amalek, what he did along the way when the children of Israel came out of Egypt, and how to treat him. "He attacked those among you in the rear, all the stragglers behind you, when you were tired and weary—he did not fear God. Now when Adonai your God grants you rest from all the enemies surrounding you in the land Adonai your God is giving you as an inheritance to possess, you are to blot out the memory of Amalek from under the heavens. Do not forget!" Deuteronomy 25:18-19

## LESSON DISCUSSION

## HOW WE TREAT EACH OTHER MATTERS TO ADONAI

### Deuteronomy 21:10 NASB
"When you go out to battle against your enemies, and the Lord your God delivers them into your hands and you take them away captive.

Our Torah Portion begins with a command for when the children of Israel go out to war, but it also emphasizes Adonai's commandments for relationships with each other and how to conduct oneself in the land to live a long and prosperous life.

Some lessons we can learn from this week's Torah Portion include; how to treat each other, whether it is a brother/sister, a stranger, a widow, an orphan, a slave, an animal, or a bird. We also learn what is acceptable in marriage relationships, and our relationship with Adonai.

### Deuteronomy 22:1-4
"You are not to watch your brother's ox or sheep going astray and ignore them—you must certainly bring them back to your brother. **2** If your brother is not near you or if you do not know him, then you should bring it into your house and it will remain with you until your brother comes searching for it and you return it to him. **3** You are to do the same with his donkey or his coat or anything lost by your brother, that may be lost by him and you find—you may not ignore them. **4** You must not watch your brother's donkey or ox fall down on the road and ignore it—you must certainly help him lift it up again.

**WHEN SOMEONE IS IN NEED:**
- Don't ignore the person when you can help
- Watch and protect what belongs to others
- Return what was lost, even if it's been a long time
- Be helpful

**Adonai gives His commandments so we can live. He desires a holy people and a holy place.**

**Deuteronomy 23:16 CJB**

For Adonai your God moves about in your camp to rescue you and to hand over your enemies to you. Therefore your camp must be a holy place. [Adonai] should not see anything indecent among you, or he will turn away from you.

**How do you treat your room? Can Adonai visit you there?**

**In our Torah reading, we see each time a punishment is established for disobedience Moses, declares against the act of disobedience:**
- It is detestable to Adonai
- To put an end to wickedness
- Do not defile the land
- Expel wickedness from Israel

**THE LITTLE THINGS MATTER - The Least of the Commandments**

**Deuteronomy 22:6-7**

"If there happens to be a bird's nest in front of you along the road, in any tree or on the ground, with young ones or eggs and the hen sitting on the young or on the eggs, you are not to take the hen with the young. **7** You must certainly let the hen go, but the young you may take for yourself so that it may go well with you and you may prolong your days.

**This commandment may seem simple or not so important. Let's hear what Yeshua has to say about the least important commandments.**

**Matthew 5:19 TLV**
Therefore, whoever breaks one of the least of these commandments, and teaches others the same, shall be called least in the kingdom of heaven. But whoever keeps and teaches them, this one shall be called great in the kingdom of heaven.

**Why do you think Adonai allows us to only take the young?**
(Give the children a chance to think and answer the question).

**Possible answer:** Adonai wants to preserve life. If the mother bird is taken before her eggs hatch then the babies might die before they hatch. The mother bird is needed for the young chicks to receive food and protect them until they can go out on their own.

**You are like a young chick and your parents are the mother bird. Would you be able to care for yourself if your parents were not a home?**

**When we do the least of the commandments Adonai promises to give us long life. It is the same promise we receive for our obedience to our parents**

**Exodus 20:12**
"Honor your father and your mother, so that your days may be long upon the land which Adonai your God is giving you.

**Deuteronomy 5:16**
Honor your father and your mother just as Adonai your God commanded you, so that your days may be long and it may go well with you in the land Adonai your God is giving you.

**Ephesians 6:1-3**

Children, obey your parents in the Lord, for this is right. **2** "Honor your father and mother" (which is the first commandment with a promise), **3** "So that it may be well with you, and you may live long on the earth."

**Proverbs 3:1-2**

My son, do not forget my teaching, but let your heart keep my mitzvot. **2** For length of days and years of life, and shalom they will add to you.

## TURNING POINT:

### REMEMBER

Moses described the various laws and rules to the children of Israel as Adonai had commanded him. This Torah Portion focuses on how to treat others and things to remember.

**The children of Israel were commanded to remember three things:**
   **1. Remember what Adonai did to Miriam**

**Deuteronomy 24:8-9**
"When there is an outbreak of tzara'at, be careful to observe and do just what the cohanim (priests), who are L'vi'im (Levites), teach you. Take care to do as I ordered them. 9 Remember what Adonai your God did to Miryam on the road after you left Egypt.

Miriam was punished with tzara'at because of lashon harah. She defied authority. The caution here is for the children of Isreal to listen and obey the priests and Levites.

   **2. Remember you were slaves in Egypt**

**Deuteronomy 24:19-22**
"When harvesting the grain in your field, if you forgot a sheaf of grain there, you are not to go back and get it; it will remain there for the foreigner, the orphan and the widow, so that Adonai your God will bless you in all the work you do. **20** When you beat your olive tree, you are not to go back over the branches again; the olives that are left will be for the foreigner, the orphan and the widow. **21** When you gather the grapes from your vineyard, you are not to return and pick grapes a second time; what is left will be for the foreigner, the orphan and the widow. **22** Remember that you were a slave in the land of Egypt. That is why I am ordering you to do this.

As slaves in Egypt, the children of Israel were treated harshly. Adonai did not want them to behave like the Egyptians with the foreigners, orphans, or widows. He wanted them to show love and kindness just as He loved to show them love and kindness.

### 3. Remember what Amalek did to you
**Deuteronomy 25:17-19**

"Remember what 'Amalek did to you on the road as you were coming out of Egypt, 18 how he met you by the road, attacked those in the rear, those who were exhausted and straggling behind when you were tired and weary. He did not fear God. **19** Therefore, when Adonai your God has given you rest from all your surrounding enemies in the land Adonai your God is giving you as your inheritance to possess, you are to blot out all memory of 'Amalek from under heaven. Don't forget!

Amalek did not fear Adonai. He did not give the children of Israel the basic needs for survival as they traveled through the wilderness, instead, Amalek attacked them.

**What are the lessons for you to learn?**
- Don't disregard the commandments of Adonai. Listen to those in authority.
- Show kindness towards others to demonstrate the love of your Father in Heaven.
- Don't associate with those who do not fear Adonai, because you will be destroyed when He seeks vengeance.

**REMEMBER: PROVERBS 3:1-2 TLV**

My son, do not forget my teaching, but let your heart keep my mitzvot. **2** For length of days and years of life, and shalom they will add to you.

## PRACTICAL APPLICATIONS

### FOR CHILDREN 5 4-6 YEARS OLD

Parents, please read Psalm 119:81-96 as a declaration over your child/children.

### FOR CHILDREN 7-12 YEARS OLD

Parents, please read Psalm 119:81-96 as a declaration over your child/children.

Children, please read three verses each night before bed from Psalm 119:81-96

### FOLLOW-UP FROM THE LAST TORAH PORTION

Ask who wants to share from last week's practical application.

### FOR CHILDREN 4-6 YEARS OLD

Parents, please read Psalm 119:65-80 as a declaration over your child/children.

### FOR CHILDREN 7-12 YEARS OLD

Parents, please read Psalm 119:65-80 as a declaration over your child/children.

Children, please read three verses each night before bed from Psalm 119:65-80.

# QUESTIONS - TEACHERS ANSWER KEY

1. **How long should a captive woman weep for her parents?**
   One month

2. **What did Adonai say about taking a bird?**
   Send her away before taking her young

3. **If a man has two sons and the older one is from the wife he hates and the younger one is from the wife he loves, which son gets the inheritance of the firstborn?**
   The firstborn son of the hated wife

4. **A person hung on a tree is <u>cursed.</u>**

5. **Why should a dead person be buried on the same day?**
   It pollutes/defiles the land

6. **What two animals should not plow together in the field?**
   Ox and donkey

7. **Why is it not permitted for a woman to wear clothes made for a man or a man to wear clothes made for a woman?**
   It is detestable to Adonai

8. **What two nations were not permitted to enter the congregation of Adonai up to the tenth generation?**
   Ammonites and Moabites

9. **Who were the children of Israel warned not to fight against?**
   Edomites and Egyptians

10. **Who should the children of Israel remember to blot out his name?**
    Amalek

# QUESTIONS - CHILDREN'S COPY

1. How long should a captive woman weep for her parents?

2. What did Adonai say about taking a bird?

3. If a man has two sons and the older one is from the wife he hates and the younger one is from the wife he loves, which son gets the inheritance of the firstborn?

4. A person hung on a tree is _____. Deut.21:23

5. Why should a dead body be buried on the same day? Deut.21:23

6. What two animals should not plow together in the field?

7. Why is it not permitted for a woman to wear clothes made for a man or a man to wear clothes made for a woman? Deut.22:5

8. What two nations were not permitted to enter the congregation of Adonai up to the tenth generation?

9. Who were the children of Israel warned not to fight against?

10. Who should the children of Israel remember to blot out his name?

# CRAFTS SUPPLIES FOR THE TORAH PORTION KI TETZE

**SUPPLIES:**
1. "12x12" Cardstock Paper
2. Print Paper
3. Brown Cardstock
4. Green Felt Fabric
5. Green Construction Paper
6. Googly Eyes
7. Coloring Pencils or Crayons
8. Brown Crinkled Paper that you Use for Stuffing
9. Glue and Glue Sticks

# CRAFTS: MAMA BIRD

1. Glue tree trunk/branches cut out on 12×12" cardstock on the left of the paper, as shown.
2. Glue green felt leaves as shown. Fold green construction paper leaves in half, then glue the bottom half of the leaves next to green felt leaves, as shown.

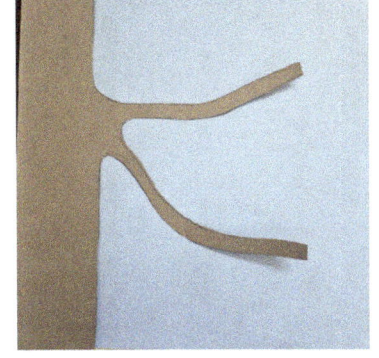

3. Color the mama bird in yellow and brown and glue her on top of the top branch.
4. Put googly eyes on the bird.

5. Color 2 baby birds and then glue them on the bottom branch as shown.
6. With a glue stick and crinkled brown paper, start building your bird nest. Glue a whole bunch on top of one another so it looks like a nest.

FINISHED WORK

# Ki Tavo

## "When You Enter"

## Torah Portion 50: Ki Tavo

This week's Torah Portion is **Ki Tavo**, translated as **"when you enter"** in the first verse of our Torah reading.

## Scripture Readings:

Deuteronomy 26:1-29:8, Isaiah 60:1-22, Matthew 4:13-24, Psalm 31

## The Theme of the Torah Portion:

Rejoice before Adonai!

## Scripture for Theme

### Deuteronomy 28:47-48

"Because you did not serve the Lord your God with joy and a glad heart, for the abundance of all things; **48** therefore you shall serve your enemies whom the Lord will send against you, in hunger, in thirst, in nakedness, and in the lack of all things; and He will put an iron yoke on your neck until He has destroyed you.

# Torah Portion Outline

- Firstfruits Offering, **Deuteronomy 26:1-4**
- Declaration for the Firstfruits, **Deuteronomy 26:5-11**
- Confessions of the Tithes, **Deuteronomy 26:12-15**
- Covenant Bond, **Deuteronomy 26:16-19**
- Torah Written on Stones, **Deuteronomy 27:1-10**
- Curses Pronounced on the Mount Ebal, **Deuteronomy 27:11-26**
- Blessings for Obeying the Commandments, **Deuteronomy 28:1-14**
- Curses for Disobeying the Commandments, **Deuteronomy 28:15-69**
- A Renewed Commitment to the Covenant at Moab, **Deuteronomy 29:1-8**

# LESSON SUMMARY

This week's Torah Portion begins "When you enter the land that Adonai your God is giving you as an inheritance...." The children of Israel were commanded to bring the first fruits of some of the fruits from the ground of the land. It describes the details of the first fruit offering that was commanded to the children of Israel in Exodus 23:19.

They were to put their first in a basket and bring it to the priest in the place where Adonai chose to put His name and say to him, "I declare today to Adonai your God, that I have entered into the land Adonai swore to our fathers to give us. Then the priest shall take the basket from your hand and set it down before the altar of the Lord your God, (Deut.26:4). The priest would take the basket and place it before the altar of Adonai. They were to make a declaration of Adonai's goodness towards their fathers remembering all that Adonia had done for them and where He brought them from. Together with the Levites and the strangers among them, they were to worship Adonia and rejoice in all His goodness.

This Torah Portion also gives the command for the tithe, the tenth of the produce of the third year. They were to bring the tithe to the Levite, the stranger in the land, the orphan, and the widow, so they may eat and be satisfied. They also were to make a declaration for the tithes, that they had obeyed the commandments of Adonai concerning the tithe; they had not eaten any of the tithes while they were in mourning, taken any from it while they were ritually unclean, or given any to the dead.

This Torah Portion also includes instructions for writing the Torah on stones, setting them on Mount Ebal, setting up stones to make an altar to worship Adonai, and proclaiming the blessings and curses on Mount Gerizim and Mount Ebal when they crossed the Jordan into the promised land. Moses told the children of Israel six tribes were to stand on Mount Gerizim to proclaim the blessings, and six tribes on Mount Ebal to proclaim the curses. The Levites should stand in the valley between the two mountains and with a loud voice saying "Cursed is the man who..." (See Deut.27:15-26 for curses).

Moses also proclaimed the blessings to the children of Israel. He said to them; Now it shall be, if you diligently obey the Lord your God, being careful to do all His commandments which I command you today, the Lord your God will set you high above all the nations of the earth. All these blessings will come upon you and overtake you if you obey the Lord your God…(Deut. 28:1-2)" (See Deut. 28:3-14 for blessings).

Moses told the children of Israel not to forget that they are a holy people separated from all nations for Adonai. He spoke to them saying; "This day the Lord your God commands you to do these statutes and ordinances. You shall therefore be careful to do them with all your heart and with all your soul. You have today declared the Lord to be your God, and that you would walk in His ways and keep His statutes, His commandments, and His ordinances, and listen to His voice. The Lord has today declared you to be His people, a treasured possession, as He promised you, and that you should keep all His commandments; and that He will set you high above all nations which He has made, for praise, fame, and honor; and that you shall be a consecrated people to the Lord your God, as He has spoken."(Deut. 26:16-19). The Torah Portion concludes with Moses reminding the children of Israel of all that Adonai had done for them the past forty (40) years in the wilderness. He confirmed with them the covenant and all the words that Adonai spoke to them in Moab as He did with their fathers in Horeb.

## LESSON DISCUSSION

### FIRST THINGS FIRST

**Deuteronomy 26:1-3**
"Then it shall be, when you enter the land which the Lord your God gives you as an inheritance, and you possess it and live in it, 2 that you shall take some of the first of all the produce of the ground which you bring in from your land that the Lord your God gives you, and you shall put it in a basket and go to the place where the Lord your God chooses to establish His name. 3 You shall go to the priest who is in office at that time and say to him, 'I declare this day to the Lord my God that I have entered the land which the Lord swore to our fathers to give us.'

**The children of Israel were to bring their firstfruit offering to Adonai who was ~~the~~ first in their lives.**

**How can you show Adonai that He is ~~the~~ first in your life?**

### MY DECLARATION

The children of Israel were also commanded to make a declaration when they brought their firstfruit offering. It was a testimony that they had received their inheritance in the land. This declaration was to remind them of their history, where Adonai had brought them from, and all that He had done for them. It was also a reminder to them that Adonai was the one who provided everything they had. The tithe was brought to the priest in the place where Adonai put His name. The priest would stand as a witness that they had done all that Adonai had commanded them to do.

**Deuteronomy 26:4-11**

Then the priest shall take the basket from your hand and set it down before the altar of the Lord your God. **5** You shall answer and say before the Lord your God, 'My father was a wandering Aramean, and he went down to Egypt and sojourned there, few in number; but there he became a great, mighty and populous nation. **6** And the Egyptians treated us harshly and afflicted us, and imposed hard labor on us. **7** Then we cried to the Lord, the God of our fathers, and the Lord heard our voice and saw our affliction and our toil and our oppression; **8** and the Lord brought us out of Egypt with a mighty hand and an outstretched arm and with great terror and with signs and wonders; **9** and He has brought us to this place and has given us this land, a land flowing with milk and honey. **10** Now behold, I have brought the first of the produce of the ground which You, O Lord have given me.' And you shall set it down before the Lord your God, and worship before the Lord your God; **11** and you and the Levite and the alien who is among you shall rejoice in all the good which the Lord your God has given you and your household.

**Yeshua is our inheritance**

Adonai gave the children of Israel the land as an inheritance when He brought them out of Egypt. Egypt for us represents a state of sin and darkness. God sent Yeshua, His son, to bring us out of sin and darkness so that we also can receive an inheritance if we believe.

**John 3:16 TLV**

For God so loved the world that He gave His one and only Son, that whoever believes in Him shall not perish but have eternal life.

Like the children of Israel, we too have to make a confession and declare that we have received our inheritance.

**1 John 1:9 TLV**

If we confess our sins, He is faithful and righteous to forgive our sins and purify us from all unrighteousness.

**Have you received your inheritance?** (At this point teacher can lead child/children into prayer of confession).

# TURNING POINT:

## CHOOSE YOUR MOUNTAIN - WALK THE TALK!

Growing up I was told by adults "Do as I say, not as I do!" It was a way of teaching me to do the right things at all times. They wanted me to learn to do right regardless of what others were doing. Was this the best way to teach me? I don't think so, but I did learn.

This, however, is not the way of the Torah. Adonai, listened to the voice of the children of Israel when they cried to Him and He did something about it. He demonstrated a principle for them and us to follow. Listen and do. Adonai desires us to not only talk about Him but to also live according to His commandments. In this week's Torah Portion, we see where Adonai commanded the children of Israel to declare what He had done for them in their obedience in bringing the firstfruit offering and tithes. Adonai also gave the children of Israel two choices; they could either obey His commandments and walk in blessings or disobey and walk in curses.

**Deuteronomy 27:11-14**
Moses also charged the people on that day, saying, **12** "When you cross the Jordan, these shall stand on Mount Gerizim to bless the people: Simeon, Levi, Judah, Issachar, Joseph, and Benjamin. **13** For the curse, these shall stand on Mount Ebal: Reuben, Gad, Asher, Zebulun, Dan, and Naphtali. 14 The Levites shall then answer and say to all the men of Israel with a loud voice.

Twelve curses are declared by the Levites and all the people say "Amen", (Deuteronomy 27:16-25). These Curses are based on their actions towards each other and God. These are the things done deliberately whether in secret or publicly.

**Deuteronomy 28:1-2**

"Now it shall be, if you diligently obey the Lord your God, being careful to do all His commandments which I command you today, the Lord your God will set you high above all the nations of the earth. 2 All these blessings will come upon you and overtake you if you obey the Lord your God."

Twelve blessings were proclaimed that the children of Israel would see in their lives if they listened to the voice of Adonai and obeyed His commandments, (Deuteronomy 28:3-14).

There were also consequences of curses if they did not obey Adonai's commandments. "But it shall come about, if you do not obey the Lord your God, to observe to do all His commandments and His statutes with which I charge you today, that all these curses will come upon you and overtake you", (Deuteronomy 28:15).

Every experience in life, good or bad, is all about choices. The choices you make today will determine the future of your life. If you want to see the blessings of Adonai in your life, you must choose the right mountain. Choose to listen and obey His commandments.

**Which mountain will you choose?**

## PRACTICAL APPLICATIONS

### FOR CHILDREN 4-6 YEARS OLD

Parents, please read Psalm 119:97-112 as a reminder of God's commandments for your child/children.

### FOR CHILDREN 7-12 YEARS OLD

Parents, please read Psalm 119:97-112 as a reminder of God's commandments for your child/children.

Children, please read three verses each night before bed from Psalm 119:97-112.

### FOLLOW-UP FROM THE LAST TORAH PORTION

Ask who wants to share from last week's practical application.

### FOR CHILDREN 4-6 YEARS OLD

Parents, please read Psalm 119:88-96 as a declaration over your child/children.

### FOR CHILDREN 7-12 YEARS OLD

Parents, please read Psalm 119:88-96 as a declaration over your child/children.

Children, please read three verses each night before bed from Psalm 119:88-96.

# QUESTIONS - TEACHERS ANSWER KEY

1. **Were the children of Israel commanded to bring an offering of all the firstfruits of the land or only some?**
   Some

2. **What were the firstfruits offerings carried in and who received them?**
   A basket, the Priest

3. **When the basket was placed before the altar of Adonai who should rejoice with the giver of the offering?**
   The Priest, the stranger, the giver, and his family

4. **What are the names of the two mountains for proclaiming curses and blessings?**
   Mount Gerizim for the blessings, and Mount Ebal for curses

5. **Who stood in the valley to declare the curses?**
   The Levites

6. **How many tribes were to stand on each mountain?**
   Six tribes on each mountain

7. **How should the children of Israel describe their father in the declaration of the firstfruits offering?**
   A wandering Aramean

8. **In what year was the tithe for the poor, stranger, and widow brought to the priest?**
   In the third year

9. **Where were the children of Israel commanded to write the Torah, and where were they set up?**
   Write on stones and set them on Mount Ebal

10. **The land of Israel is described as a land** flowing with milk and honey.

# QUESTIONS - CHILDREN'S COPY

1. Were the children of Israel commanded to bring an offering of all the firstfruits of the land or only some?

2. What were the firstfruits offerings carried in and who received them?

3. When the basket was placed before the altar of Adonai who should rejoice with the giver of the offering?

4. What are the names of the two mountains for proclaiming curses and blessings?

5. Who stood in the valley to declare the curses?

6. How many tribes were to stand on each mountain?

7. How should the children of Israel describe their father in the declaration of the firstfruits offering?

8. In what year was the tithe for the poor, stranger, and widow brought to the priest?

9. Where were the children of Israel commanded to write the Torah, and where were they set up?

10. The land of Israel is described as a land _____ _____ _____ and _____.

# CRAFTS SUPPLIES FOR TORAH PORTION KI TAVO

**SUPPLIES:**
1. "12×12" Cardstock of any color
2. "12×12" Orange Cardstock
3. White Cardstock
4. Gluestick
5. Markers, Pencils, and Crayons
6. Gems

## CRAFTS: FIRSTFRUITS

1. Put glue on one side of the cardstock basket as shown. Leave the top part of the basket open so you can put fruits in it.
2. Glue the basket on 12×12" cardstock.

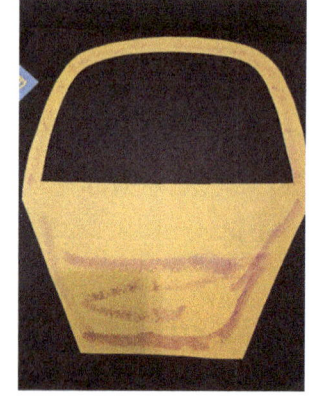

3. Ask the children to identify the 4 species of fruit they will receive. (Pomegranates and Grapes are easier than Dates and Figs).

4. Color each fruit and then place them in the basket!
5. Decorate the basket with gems.

FINAL ARTWORK

# Nitzavim-Vayelech

## "Standing-He Went"

# Torah Portion 51 & 52: Nitzavim-Vayelech

The title for this week's Torah Portion is Nitzavim—Vayelech. It is a double Torah reading. **Nitzavim** is the Hebrew word translated as **"standing"**. It is found in Deuteronomy 29:9. **Vayelech** is the Hebrew word translated as **"He went."** It is found in Deuteronomy 31:1.

## Deuteronomy 29:9 TLV
"You are **standing** today, all of you, before Adonai your God—the heads of your tribes, your elders, your officials, all the men of Israel,"

## Deuteronomy 31:1 TLV
Then "**Moses went**" and spoke these words to all Israel."

## Scripture Readings:

### Nitzavim - Standing
Deuteronomy 29:9-30:20, Isaiah 61:10-63:9, John 12:41-50, Psalm 81

### Vayelech - He went
Deuteronomy 31:1-30, Hosea 14:1-10, Hebrews 13:5-8, Psalm 65

## The Theme of the Torah Portion:

Standing In Covenant

## Scripture for Theme

### Deuteronomy 29:13-14
Not with you alone am I cutting this covenant and this oath, **14** but with whomever is standing here with us today before Adonai our God and with whomever is not here with us today.

# Torah Portion Outline

- A Covenant for Every Generation, **Deuteronomy 29:9-14**
- Guard Your Heart against Poison Roots and Bitter Fruits, **Deuteronomy 29:15-17**
- Be Aware of Pride, **Deuteronomy 29:18-20**
- Punishment for Abandoning Adonai, **Deuteronomy 29:21-28**
- When You Return to Adonai, **Deuteronomy 30:1-6**
- Curses on Your Enemies, **Deuteronomy 30:7-10**
- Heaven and Earth a Witness, **Deuteronomy 30:11-20**
- Be Courageous, **Deuteronomy 31:1-8**
- Public Reading of Torah, **Deuteronomy 31:9-18**
- A Song of Witness, **Deuteronomy 31:19-30**

# LESSON SUMMARY

In the Torah Portion Nitzavim, Moses tells the children of Israel that the Covenant of Adonai is not only for those who were standing before him but also for future generations. All those who heard the words of Adonai and chose to obey would receive the same promise of the covenant blessings for obedience, or curses for disobedience. Moses told them that everyone standing before Adonai, the leaders of their tribes, elders, officials, all the men, their children, their wives, the outsiders in the camp, and those who cut wood or draw water for them; everyone is to cross over into the covenant that Adonai is making with them.

Moses warned the children of Israel to be aware of anyone among them, whether a man or woman or a family or tribe, whose heart turns away from serving Adonai. This would produce a poisonous root and bitter fruit toward Adonai. Moses also warned of someone who had a stubborn heart and chose not to follow Adonai's ways while still believing he would be in peace and receive blessings from Adonai; such a person would suffer. Adonai's anger and jealousy would rise against him. Adonai would single him out from all the tribes of Israel and he would experience calamities. Adonai would be unwilling to forgive him.

Moses also spoke of a time when the children of Israel would be driven from the land and scattered to other nations. All the plagues and curses of the covenant would be on them and the land would burn like Sodom, Gomorrah, Admah, and Zeboiim. The nations would ask, why has Adonai done this to the land? "Then they will say, 'Because they abandoned the covenant of Adonai, the God of their fathers, which He cut with them when He brought them out from the land of Egypt. They went and served other gods and bowed down to them—gods they never knew, that He had not allotted to them. So Adonai's anger burned against that land, bringing on it every curse written in this scroll" (Deuteronomy 29:24-26).

The commandments Moses said to them are not too hard or too far for them (Deuteronomy 30:1-3). It is near in their mouths and their hearts. Moses describes the commandments of Adonai as life and good, and death and evil. Moses said to the children of Israel: "See, I have set before you today life and good, and death and evil. "I call the heavens and the earth to witness about you today, that I have set before you life and death, the blessing and the curse. Therefore choose life so that you and your descendants may live," (Deuteronomy 30:15 & 19).

In the Torah Portion, Vayelech, Moses told the people, "I am now 120 years old." Moses was no longer allowed to lead the people because it was almost time for him to die, (Deuteronomy 31:1-2). He reminded them it was Adonai who was crossing over the Jordan before them. He would destroy the nations before them, so they should not be afraid, but strong and courageous. Joshua would lead them, and go before them as a leader just as Adonai promised. Moses wrote the words of the Torah on a scroll. He gave it to the Levites who carried the Ark of the Covenant of Adonai to place in the Ark to keep it safe. Moses commanded that the Torah should be read during the Feast of Sukkot at the end of every seven years when all debts are canceled. It should be read for all the people to hear.

Adonai told Moses his time to die was near. Moses was told to call Joshua and to come to the Tent of Meeting where Adonai would commission him to lead the people. Moses and Joshua went to the Tent of Meeting. Adonai appeared in the Tent in a pillar of cloud at the entrance of the Tent of Meeting. Adonai told Moses, that there will come a day when the children of Israel will turn their backs on Him and serve foreign gods of the land they are entering. Adonai said; "Then My anger will flare against them on that day, and I will abandon them and hide My face from them. So they will be devoured, and many evils and troubles will come on them. They will say on that day, 'Isn't it because our God is not among us that these evils have come on us?' 18 I will surely hide My face on that day because of all the evil they have done, for they have turned to other gods" (Deuteronomy 31:17-18).

Moses was commanded to write a song and teach it to the children of Israel. It would be a witness for Adonai against the children of Israel. Adonai declared that because of the evil done by the people, He would hide His face from them. Moses wrote the words of the song as Adonai commanded and taught it to the people. He gave the scroll of the Torah to the Levites for them to place it in the Ark of the Covenant. Moses then gathered all the elders of the tribes and officials and spoke all the words of Adonai as a witness against them.

# LESSON DISCUSSION

**Deuteronomy 29:9-14 TLV**
"You are standing today, all of you, before Adonai your God—the heads of your tribes, your elders, your officials, all the men of Israel, **10** your children, your wives, and the outsider within your camp (from your woodchopper to your water carrier). **11** Each of you is to cross over into the covenant of Adonai your God that He is cutting with you today, and into His oath. **12** "This is in order to confirm you today as His people. So He will be your God, just as He promised you and just as He swore to your fathers—to Abraham, to Isaac and to Jacob. **13** Not with you alone am I cutting this covenant and this oath, **14** but with whomever is standing here with us today before Adonai our God and with whomever is not here with us today.

**STANDING IN COVENANT WITH ADONAI**
- Those standing before Moses: heads of tribes, elders, officials, all men, Women, Children, Wives
- The Outsider in the camp (those who serve you: Woodcutters and Water carriers)
- Those not standing there

**We have a responsibility to respond to the Word of Adonai. How will you respond TODAY?**

**TODAY** is the "**day**" we hear Adonai's Words
**Hebrew 3:14-15**
For we have become partners of Messiah, if we hold our original conviction firm until the end. **15** As it is said, "Today if you hear His voice, do not harden your hearts as in the rebellion."

**In Torah Portion Shoftim (Judges) we learned that a witness is only established by two or more (Deuteronomy 17:60). This week's Torah reading mentions three witnesses. Adonai Keeps His word!**

**WITNESSES TO THE COVENANT:**

1. Torah as witness of the promise Adonai made to Abraham, Isaac, and Jacob. Deuteronomy 29:11-12, Deuteronomy 31:25-26

2. Heaven and Earth, a witness for Moses that he has declared all the words of the Commandments of Adonai to the children of Israel. Deuteronomy 29:19-20

3. A Song, a witness for Adonai against the children of Israel when they turn their back on Him. Deuteronomy 31:19-21

**Each person is to cross over into the Covenant of Adonai. For the children of Israel crossing over into the covenant consisted of two things:**

1. They had to declare Adonai as their God and follow His commandments

2. They had to cross over the Jordan and possess the land

**How do we cross over into the covenant of Adonai today? Our crossing over also consists of two things:**

**1. We must believe in Yeshua and confess He is the Son of God.**

**Romans 10:9-13 TLV**
For if you confess with your mouth that Yeshua is Lord, and believe in your heart that God raised Him from the dead, you will be saved. **10** For with the heart it is believed for righteousness, and with the mouth it is confessed for salvation. **11** For the Scripture says, "Whoever trusts in Him will not be put to shame." **12** For there is no distinction between Jew and Greek, for the same Lord is Lord of all—richly generous to all who call on Him. **13** For "Everyone who calls upon the name of Adonai shall be saved."

## 2. We must obey the Commandments of Adonai.

### Matthew 5:17
"Do not think that I came to abolish the Torah or the Prophets! I did not come to abolish, but to fulfill.

### 1 Corinthians 7:19
Circumcision is nothing and uncircumcision is nothing—but keeping God's commandments matters.

### James 1:22-24
But be doers of the word, and not hearers only, deluding yourselves. **23** For if anyone is a hearer of the word and not a doer, he is like a man who looks at his natural face in a mirror— **24** for once he looks at himself and goes away, he immediately forgets what sort of person he was.

**Are you standing in Covenant with Adonai?**

# TURNING POINT:

## Sing Me A Song

**Deuteronomy 31:19-22**
"Now, write this song for yourselves, and teach it to Bnei-Yisrael—put it in their mouth, so that this song may be a witness for Me against Bnei-Yisrael. **20** "For when I bring them to the land flowing with milk and honey that I swore to their fathers, and they eat and are satisfied and grow fat—then they will turn to other gods and serve them, and they will spurn Me and break My covenant. **21** Now when many evils and troubles have come on them, this song will confront them as a witness; for it will not be forgotten from the mouth of their descendants. For I know the intention they are devising this day, even before I bring them into the land that I swore." **22** That day Moses wrote this song and taught it to Bnei-Yisrael.

In this week's Torah Portion of Vayelech, Adonai commands Moses to write a song. It would be a witness for Adonai against the children of Israel when they turned away from Adonai and worshiped foreign gods. Adonai had already given Moses all His commandments for the children of Israel and commanded him to write the Torah on a scroll. Moses commanded the children of Israel to write the Torah on Stones when they crossed the Jordan and set it on Mount Ebal. Stones with the Torah were also set up east of the Jordan before crossing over. The words of the Torah were everywhere for them to see. Well not everyone. Why would Adonai need a song to be a witness for Him?

When the children of Israel crossed the Reed Sea, they sang to Adonai a new song (Exodus 15). They sang of His goodness towards them and all He did to deliver them from the Egyptians. They sang of how he drowned Pharaoh and his army, and his horses and chariots. A song to the children of Israel was a declaration of Adonai's power. A song has the power to keep words as the Torah mentions in our mouths, Deuteronomy 31:19. But not just in our mouths, but in our hearts as well. Adonai wants us to have the words of the Torah written on our hearts. We cannot physically write them in our hearts. Singing is one way of writing the words of the Torah on our hearts. This is why reading of the Torah is chanted as a song among the Jewish people today.

The song you sing is important to Adonai. What we sing will be written on your heart. Your song will either speak of the goodness of Adonai or other gods. Choose today to only write the words of Adonai on your heart with a song.

**Will you sing to Adonai?**

**PRACTICAL APPLICATIONS**

### FOR CHILDREN 4-6 YEARS OLD

Parents, please read Psalm 119:113—128 as a reminder of God's commandments for your child/children.

### FOR CHILDREN 7-12 YEARS OLD

Parents, please read Psalm 119:113-128 as a reminder of God's commandments for your child/children.

Children, please read three verses each night before bed from Psalm 119:113-128.


### FOLLOW-UP FROM THE LAST TORAH PORTION

Ask who wants to share from last week's practical application.

### FOR CHILDREN 4-6 YEARS OLD

Parents, please read Psalm 119:97-112 as a reminder of God's commandments for your child/children.

### FOR CHILDREN 7-12 YEARS OLD

Parents, please read Psalm 119:97-112 as a reminder of God's commandments for your child/children.

Children, please read three verses each night before bed from Psalm 119:97-112.

# QUESTIONS - TEACHERS ANSWER KEY

1. **How old was Moses?**
   120 years old

2. **Who were some of the people standing before Moses and Adonai?**
   The heads of tribes, elders, officials, all men, Women, Children, Wives, The Outsider in the camp (those who serve you: Woodcutters and Water carriers)

3. **With whom did Adonai make His covenant?**
   Those standing before Moses and those not standing there

4. **Who did Adonai commission as Israel's new leader?**
   Joshua

5. **What did Moses call as a witness against Israel?**
   Heaven and Earth

6. **What did Adonai set as a witness for Him against Israel?**
   A Song

7. **Where was the Torah scroll placed for safekeeping?**
   In the Ark of the Covenant of Adonai

8. **How did Moses describe the commandments of Adonai?**
   Life and good, and death and evil

9. **Who will Adonai be unwilling to forgive?**
   A person who chooses not to obey and thinks in his heart he will be blessed. (A prideful person)

10. **When should the Torah be read in public for everyone to hear?**
    End of the seven years when debts are canceled, during the Feast of Sukkot

# QUESTIONS - CHILDREN'S COPY

1. How old was Moses?

2. Who were some of the people standing before Moses and Adonai?

3. With whom did Adonai make His covenant?

4. Who did Adonai commission as Israel's new leader?

5. What did Moses call as a witness against Israel?

6. What did Adonai set as a witness for Him against Israel?

7. Where was the Torah scroll placed for safekeeping?

8. How did Moses describe the commandments of Adonai?

9. Who will Adonai be unwilling to forgive?

10. Name two cities mentioned in the Torah portion as an example of Adonai's burning anger.

# CRAFTS SUPPLIES FOR TORAH PORTION NITZAVIM-VAYELECH

**SUPPLIES:**
1. Paper Plates
2. White Printing Paper
3. Pencils, Markers, Crayons
4. Orange Cardstock
5. Paper Fasteners
6. Glue or Gluesticks

# CRAFTS: CHOOSE LIFE

1. Color the wheel. Each triangle has a different color.
2. Pull paper fasteners through the 3 layers: the orange arrow, the paper wheel, and the paper plate. Fasten in the back. Holes are already punched.
3. Secure the wheel with some glue or glue stick so it's secure on a plate.

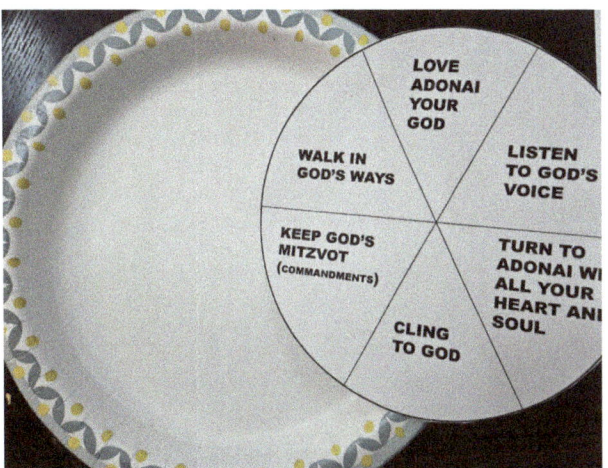

4. Color and Glue the header on top "To Choose Life"
5. Write "I must on the arrow"
6. Decorate the paper plate.

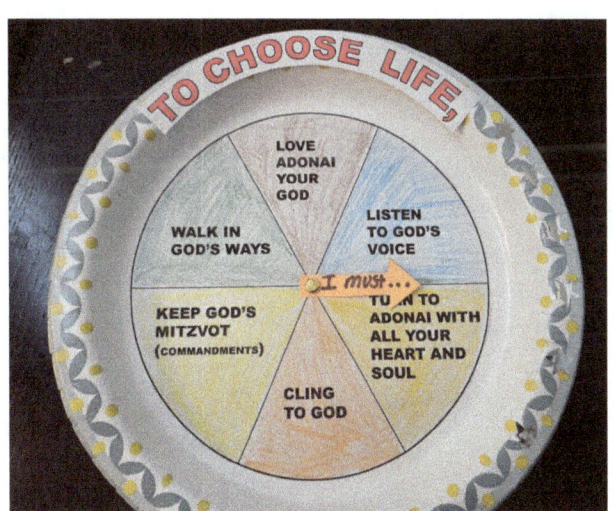

*IF TIME PERMITS, PLAY A GAME.

Roll a dice. Move the arrow clockwise to the number of spots of the number on the dice. Explain in your own words, what this means to you.

# Ha'azinu

## "Hear"

# Torah Portion 53: Ha'azinu

The title of this week's Torah Portion is **"Ha'azinu"**. It is the Hebrew word translated as **"give ear"** in our Torah reading. It is found in Deuteronomy 32:1.

## Deuteronomy 32:1 TLV

"**Give ear**, O heavens, and I will speak!
Let the earth hear the words of my mouth.

## Scripture Readings:

Deuteronomy 32:1-52, 2Samuel 22:1-22, Micah 7:18-20, Matthew 18:21-35, Psalm 71

## The Theme of the Torah Portion:

God is worthy of Praise

## Scripture for Theme

## Deuteronomy 32:3-4 NASB

"For I proclaim the name of the Lord; Ascribe greatness to our God! **4** "The Rock! His work is perfect, For all His ways are just; A God of faithfulness and without injustice, Righteous and upright is He.

# Torah Portion Outline

- The Song of Moses, **Deuteronomy 32:1-43**
- The Words of the Song In Your Heart, **Deuteronomy 32:44-47**
- Moses Sees the Land from Afar, **Deuteronomy 32:45-52**

# LESSON SUMMARY

In the last Torah Portion, Vayelech, Adonai commanded Moses to write a song that would be a witness for Him against the children of Israel. It would be a witness for Adonai against the children of Israel when they turned away from Adonai and worshiped foreign gods. In this week's Torah Portion, Moses wrote the song and taught it to the children of Israel. The words of the song call heaven and earth to be witness to Moses' words as he declared the name of Adonai. The song spoke of Adonai's faithfulness and His righteousness. Moses told the children of Israel to remember the days of past generations. He said to them, "Ask your father, and he will inform you, Your elders, and they will tell you. "When the Most High gave the nations their inheritance, When He separated the sons of man, He set the boundaries of the peoples According to the number of the sons of Israel. "For the Lord's portion is His people; Jacob is the allotment of His inheritance." (Deuteronomy 32:7b-9 NASB).

The song also speaks of a time when the children of Israel would forget about Adonai and make Him jealous by serving strange gods and turning their backs on Him. "Jeshurun *(Israel)* grew fat and kicked—You are grown fat, thick, and sleek—Then he forsook God who made him, And scorned the Rock of his salvation" (Deuteronomy 32;15). Adonai would judge them for their sins. "Then He said, 'I will hide My face from them, I will see what their end shall be; For they are a perverse generation, Sons in whom is no faithfulness. 'They have made Me jealous with what is not god; They have provoked Me to anger with their idols. So I will make them jealous with those who are not a people; I will provoke them to anger with a foolish nation, For a fire is kindled in My anger, And burns to the lowest part of Sheol, And consumes the earth with its yield, And sets on fire the foundations of the mountains" (Deuteronomy 32:20-22 NASB).

Moses and Joshua taught the words of the song to the children of Israel. After Moses finished speaking all the words of the song to the children of Israel, he said to them, "Take to your heart all the words with which I am warning you today, which you shall command your sons to observe carefully, even all the words of this law. For it is not an idle word for you; indeed it is your life. And by this word you will prolong your days in the land, which you are about to cross the Jordan to possess" (Deuteronomy 32:46-47).

Moses was then commanded to go up to the mountain of Avirm, Mount Nebo. It is the land facing Jericho. There he could see the land of Canaan which Adonai was giving the children of Israel to possess. Moses would see the land from afar, but would not enter into the land. On the mountain, Adonai said, Moses would be gathered to his people just as Aaron his brother died on Mount Hor and was gathered to his people.

# LESSON DISCUSSION

## The Song of Moses

In last week's Torah Portion of Vayelech Adonai commanded Moses to write a song. It would be a witness for Adonai against the children of Israel when they turned away from Adonai and worshiped foreign gods. In this Torah Portion, Moses writes the song Adonai commanded him to write, Deuteronomy 31:19-22. He and Joshua taught the song to the children of Israel.

## Deuteronomy 32:1-4

"Give ear, O heavens, and let me speak; And let the earth hear the words of my mouth. **2** "Let my teaching drop as the rain, My speech distill as the dew, As the droplets on the fresh grass And as the showers on the herb. **3** "For I proclaim the name of the Lord; Ascribe greatness to our God! **4** "The Rock! His work is perfect, For all His ways are just; A God of faithfulness and without injustice, Righteous and upright is He.

The song of Moses is more than just words and a melody. It is a declaration of who Adonai is to the children of Israel. A recalling of what He did for them. A proclamation of Israel's future rejection of Adonai. Adonai's mercy towards them despite their rejection. Adonai's unending love toward the children of Israel. The Song of Moses is also a song of Reconciliation for all nations.

## THE SONG AT A GLANCE

- Moses Calls Heaven and Earth as Witnesses, **Deuteronomy 32:1-4**
- Israel Breaks Covenant with Adonai, **Deuteronomy 32:5-6**
- Moses Recalls all Adonai did for Israel, **Deuteronomy 32:7-14**
- Israel Rejects Adonai, **Deuteronomy 32:15-18**
- Adonai's Response to Israel's Rejection, **Deuteronomy 32:19-26**
- Adonai's Mercy Towards Israel, **Deuteronomy 32:27-43**

- Moses Instructs the People to Teach the Song to Their Children, **Deuteronomy 32:44-47**
- Moses Commanded to go to Mount Nebo, **Deuteronomy 32:48-52**

**Moses declares the attributes of Adonai in his song; Great, Rock, Blameless, Just, Faithful, Righteous, and Father. We can rely on Adonai to be our God and Father.**

### WHY DID MOSES CALL HEAVEN AND EARTH TO BE HIS WITNESS?

No matter where the children of Israel went there will always be a witness that they belong to Adonai. They are His inheritance forever.

### Psalm 19:2-5 TLV

The heavens declare the glory of God, and the sky shows His handiwork. **3** Day to day they speak, night to night they reveal knowledge. **4** There is no speech, no words, where their voice goes unheard. **5** Their voice has gone out to all the earth and their words to the end of the world.

### Always A Father!

Adonai is a Father to Israel, even when they reject Him. They will always be His people even when He is angry with them because of their actions. As a loving Father, He disciplines them to bring them back into covenant with Him.

### Deuteronomy 32:5-6

They have acted corruptly toward Him, They are not His children, because of their defect; But are a perverse and crooked generation. 6 "Do you thus repay the Lord, O foolish and unwise people? Is not He your Father who has bought you? He has made you and established you.

**Do you think your parents stop loving you when they discipline you?**

Parents sometimes get angry when you don't obey them, but that does not mean they do not love you. They will always love you, but they are angry when your choices reject what they teach you. In love, they discipline you, and so too, Adonai disciplines His children when they disobey His commandments. Moses declared in the song "Yes, God will judge his people, but oh how compassionately he'll do it," Deuteronomy 32:36 MSG.

**Will You Remember?**

**Everything Adonai does is a demonstration of His love.**

When Adonai turned His face from Israel because of their sins, their enemies would rise up against them. Adonai would rescue His people and avenge them of their enemies. He does not want the enemies to get the wrong idea gloating and saying; "we have conquered them by our power, God did not do this." Deuteronomy 32:27

**Micah 7:18-20**

Who is a God like You pardoning iniquity, overlooking transgression, for the remnant of His heritage? He will not retain His anger forever, because He delights in mercy. **19** He will again have compassion on us. He will subdue our iniquities, and You will cast all our sins into the depths of the sea. **20** You will extend truth to Jacob, mercy to Abraham, that You swore to our ancestors from the days of old.

**Romans 2:4 The Voice**

Do you take the kindness of God for granted? Do you see His patience and tolerance as signs that He is a pushover when it comes to sin? How could you not know that His kindness is guiding our hearts to turn away from distractions and habitual sin to walk a new path?

**A Song of Reconciliation. Our relationship with Adonai is reconciled (restored) through Yeshua.**

### Romans 5:6-11

For while we were still helpless, at the right time Messiah died for the ungodly. **7** For rarely will anyone die for a righteous man— though perhaps for a good man someone might even dare to die. **8** But God demonstrates His own love toward us, in that while we were yet sinners, Messiah died for us. **9** How much more then, having now been set right by His blood, shall we be saved from God's wrath through Him. **10** For if, while we were yet enemies, we were reconciled to God through the death of His Son, how much more, having been reconciled, shall we be saved by His life. **11** And not only that, but we also boast in God through our Lord Yeshua the Messiah, through whom we have now received reconciliation.

# TURNING POINT:

## Ascribe greatness to our God!

In the first fourteen verses of our Torah reading, Moses declared the greatness of God towards the children of Israel and recalls His mighty works towards them. He challenged them to remember all that Adonai had done for them from the days of Adam throughout all generations.

**Deuteronomy 32:7-12 CJB**
"Remember how the old days were; think of the years through all the ages. Ask your father — he will tell you; your leaders too — they will inform you. **8** "When 'Elyon gave each nation its heritage, when he divided the human race, he assigned the boundaries of peoples according to Isra'el's population; **9** but Adonai's share was his own people, Ya'akov his allotted heritage. **10** "He found his people in desert country, in a howling, wasted wilderness. He protected him and cared for him, guarded him like the pupil of his eye, **11** like an eagle that stirs up her nest, hovers over her young, spreads out her wings, takes them and carries them as she flies. **12** "Adonai alone led his people; no alien god was with him.

When we remember what Adonai has done for us it is easy to praise Him and ascribe greatness to His name. In everything, our first response is to ascribe greatness to God. Learn to praise God when things are going well and when things are not going well.

Sometimes it is not easy to think of words to praise Adonai, but we can learn from King David who praised Adonai using His words from the Torah. David declares; "Adonai is my rock, my fortress and my deliverer. My God is my rock, in Him I take refuge, my shield, my horn of salvation, my stronghold and my refuge, my Savior—You save me from violence. I called upon Adonai, worthy of praise, and I was rescued from my enemies," (2 Samuel 22:2-4).

A great way to learn to sing praise to Adonai is to write verses from the Book of Psalms that declare praises to Him and read them every day.

**Let's practice with a verse from our Psalm for this week.**

**Psalm 71:3 NASB**

Be to me a rock of habitation to which I may continually come; You have given commandment to save me, For You are my rock and my fortress.

## PRACTICAL APPLICATIONS

### FOR CHILDREN 4-6 YEARS OLD

Parents, please read Psalm 119:129-152 as a reminder of God's commandments for your child/children.

### FOR CHILDREN 7-12 YEARS OLD

Parents, please read Psalm 119:129-152 as a reminder of God's commandments for your child/children.

Children, please read three verses each night before bed from Psalm 119:129-152. Then write two verses from the reading that ascribe greatness to Adonai. Study and memorize them.

## FOLLOW-UP FROM THE LAST TORAH PORTION

Ask who wants to share from last week's practical application.

### FOR CHILDREN 4-6 YEARS OLD

Parents, please read Psalm 119:113-128 as a reminder of God's commandments for your child/children.

### FOR CHILDREN 7-12 YEARS OLD

Parents, please read Psalm 119:113-128 as a reminder of God's commandments for your child/children.

Children, please read three verses each night before bed from Psalm 119:113-128.

# QUESTIONS - TEACHERS ANSWER KEY

**1. What name did Moses call Israel when they grew fat? Deut.32:15**

Jeshurun

**2. Who is Adonai's inheritance?**

The Children of Israel

**3. On what mountain was Moses commanded to go up to see the land?**

Mount Nebo

**4. Give ear O <u>heavens</u>, and I will speak! Deut.32:1**

**5. Let the <u>earth</u> hear the <u>words</u> of my mouth. Deut.32:1**

**6. Who taught the song to the children of Israel?**

Moses and Joshua

**7. Moses declares I will <u>proclaim</u> Adonai's Name and ascribe <u>greatness</u> to our God. Deut.32:3**

**8. Adonai spreads his wings like an <u>eagle</u> over Israel. Deut. 32:11**

**9. How did the children of Israel make Adonai jealous?**

By serving foreign gods

**10. By whom is our relationship reconciled (restored) to Adonai?**

Through Yeshua

# QUESTIONS - CHILDREN'S COPY

1. What name did Moses call Israel when they grew fat? Deut.32:15

2. Who is Adonai's inheritance?

3. On what mountain was Moses commanded to go up to see the land?

4. Give ear O _____, and I will speak! Deut.32:1

5. Let the _____ hear the _____ of my mouth. Deut.32:1

6. Who taught the song to the children of Israel?

7. Moses declares I will _____ Adonai's Name and ascribe _____ to our God. Deut.32:3

8. Adonai spreads his wings like an _____ over Israel. Deut. 32:11

9. How did the children of Israel make Adonai jealous?

10. By whom is our relationship reconciled (restored) to Adonai?

# CRAFTS SUPPLIES FOR TORAH PORTION HA'AZINU

**SUPPLIES:**
1. Paper Plates
2. Cotton Balls
3. Print Paper
4. Cardstock
5. Pens or Pencils
6. Color Pencils or Crayons
7. Color Yarn
8. Scotch Tape
9. Glue and Glue Stick

**CRAFTS:**

1. Each child will receive a cut out of the cloud made from a paper plate.
2. Color the Repentance cloud sign and glue it on top of the plate.
3. Glue cotton balls to represent the cloud.

4. Fill out 4 Repentance raindrop cards! Some children might need help writing them out.
5. Color them with pencils or crayons.

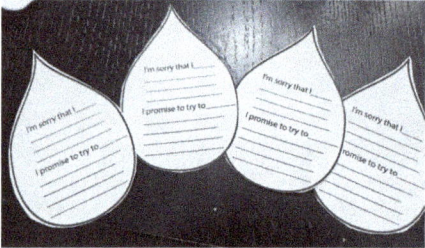 

6. Take 4 pieces of yarn and attach one to the raindrops. Then attach the other end of the yarn to the clouds as shown.

THE FINAL WORK!

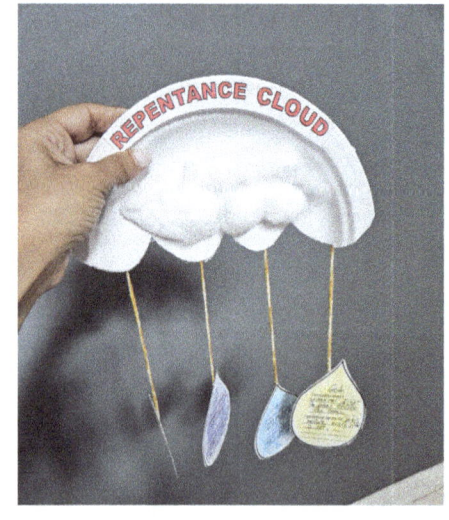

# Vezot-Ha'Bracha

## "This is the Blessing"

## Torah Portion 54: Vezot-Ha'Bracha

The title of this week's Torah Portion is called **"Vezot Ha'Brachah."** It is the Hebrew phrase translated as **"this is the Blessing"** in the Torah reading.

**Deuteronomy 33:1**
This is the blessing with which Moses the man of God blessed Bnei-Yisrael before his death.

## Scripture Readings:

Deuteronomy 33:1-34:12, Joshua 1:1-18, Acts 1:1-14, Psalm 12

# The Theme of the Torah Portion:

A Blessed Family

## Scripture for Theme

**Deuteronomy 33:29**

Happy are you, O Israel! Who is like you, a people saved by the Lord, the shield of your help, and the sword of your triumph! Your enemies shall come fawning to you, and you shall tread upon their backs."

# Torah Portion Outline

- Moses Blesses the twelve tribes of Israel, **Deuteronomy 33:1-29**
- The Death of Moses, **Deuteronomy 34:1-8**
- Joshua Leads the People, **Deuteronomy 34:9-12**

# LESSON SUMMARY

In the last Torah Portion, Ha'azinu, Moses wrote his song and taught it to the children of Israel. The Torah Portion Ha'azinu ended with the command for Moses to ascend to Mount Nebo where he would see the Promised Land of Canaan from afar. Moses would not enter the land because he did not obey Adonai when he was told to speak to the rock for the children of Israel to get water to drink. Instead of speaking to the rock, he hit the rock with his rod and called the children of Israel rebels.

In this week's Torah Portion, Moses spoke his final words before his death. Moses declared a blessing on the children of Israel. Each of the twelve tribes received their blessing. Even the sons of Joseph were included in the blessing Moses declared over Israel.

After Moses blessed the children of Israel, he ascended to Mount Nebo. There Adonai showed him all the land of Israel's inheritance. Moses died on the mountain. Adonai buried him in the valley in the land of Moab. No one knows where he was buried, because Adonai hid him. Moses was 120 years old when he died. His eyesight was not dim, nor did he lose his strength. The children of Israel mourned the death of Moses for thirty days, for it was the allotted time for mourning for the dead. Joshua was filled with the Spirit of wisdom because Moses laid his hands on him, and led the children of Israel into the land. All of Israel listened to him just as Adonai commanded.

The Torah ends with this declaration "There has not risen again in Israel a prophet in Israel like Moses with whom Adonai knew face to face" (Deuteronomy 34:11).

*We have completed the final book in the Torah.*
*Chazak chazak v'nitchazek! Be Strong, be strong, and may you be strengthened!*

## LESSON DISCUSSION

**A Blessing for Everyone**

Moses declared a blessing on the children of Israel. Though he declared a blessing for each tribe, his blessing was not intended to separate them but to unite them in their strengths.

Each tribe's blessing was a gift that was to help everyone so that Israel could stand strong as a nation. Their blessings serve as a guide for the responsibility of each tribe. Adonai revealed Himself to the children of Israel. They accepted His word and received a blessing as a part of their reward.

**Deuteronomy 33:6-29**
- Reuben is blessed with a long life
- Judah is blessed as a warrior to help his brothers
- Levi is given the blessing of righteousness judgment from the Torah with the Thummim and Your Urim. They will teach their brothers the commandments of Adonai
- Benjamin is the most loved of the Lord. He will dwell in safety
- Joseph received a blessing from the bounty (reward) of heaven. His sons Ephraim and Manasseh will spread throughout all the nations of the earth
- Zebulun will rejoice in his going out
- Issachar rejoices in his tents with the abundance of the seas and hidden treasure of the sand
- Gad is blessed by his brothers. He dwells as a lion
- Dan is a lion's cub leaping out of Bashan
- Naphtali satisfied with favor, and full of blessings from Adonai, possesses the sea and the south
- Asher most blessed of the sons, the favorite of his brothers. He dips his foot in oil. His sandals will be of iron and bronze. He will be as strong all the days of his life

**Can you think of a moment when your dad or mom said something special about you? How did you feel when you heard their words?**

**You are special to Adonai. He has promises and blessings for you if you choose to serve Him. God gives us everything we need when we put our hope and trust in Yeshua (Jesus).**

### Ephesians 1:3-7

Blessed be the God and Father of our Lord Yeshua the Messiah, who has blessed us with every spiritual blessing in the heavenly places in Messiah. **4** He chose us in the Messiah before the foundation of the world, to be holy and blameless before Him in love. **5** He predestined us for adoption as sons through Messiah Yeshua, in keeping with the good pleasure of His will— **6** to the glorious praise of His grace, with which He favored us through the One He loves! **7** In Him we have redemption through His blood—the removal of trespasses—in keeping with the richness of His grace

### 2 Peter 1:1-3 TLV

To those who have received a faith equal to ours through the righteousness of our God and Savior, Messiah Yeshua: **2** May grace and shalom be multiplied to you in the knowledge of God and of Yeshua our Lord. 3 His divine power has given us everything we need for life and godliness, through the knowledge of Him who called us by His own glory and virtue.

**God also blesses us with gifts to help each other!**

### Ephesians 4:11-13 NASB

And He gave some as apostles, some as prophets, some as evangelists, some as pastors and teachers, **12** for the equipping of the saints for the work of ministry, for the building up of the body of Christ; **13** until we all attain to the unity of the faith, and of the knowledge of the Son of God, to a mature man, to the measure of the stature which belongs to the fullness of Christ.

When Adonai blesses us it is to help others so they can grow and experience His love. Our gifts are to be used to share the good news about Yeshua and the Kingdom of God.

**Do you want to be used by Adonai?**

(Teacher: use this time to pray with the children)

# TURNING POINT:

## A Gift from God!

In this week's Torah Portion, we are told Moses died at 120 years old. When he heard God speak to him from the burning bush Moses was 80 years old. That day changed his life forever. Forty years later he is known as the most humble man and a great prophet because he listened and obeyed the voice of God. Moses had a close relationship with God. You too, can have a close relationship with Him if you choose to listen to His voice and obey.

Samuel the prophet served in the Temple when he was a young boy. "Samuel ministered before Adonai, as a boy girded with a linen ephod. His mother would make him a little robe and bring it to him from year to year when she would come up with her husband to offer the annual sacrifice" 1 Samuel 2:18-19.

He was blessed with the gift of hearing God's voice. Adonai spoke to him and gave him a message to give Eli the priest.

### 1 Samuel 3:3-10

Samuel was lying down in Adonai's Temple, where the ark of God was. **4** Then Adonai called, "Samuel!" So he answered, "Here I am." **5** Then he ran to Eli and said, "Here I am, for you called me." But he replied, "I didn't call—go back to sleep." So he went back and lay down. **6** Then Adonai called Samuel yet again. So Samuel arose and went to Eli, and said, "Here I am, for you called me." But he answered, "I didn't call, my son—go back to sleep." **7** Now Samuel had not experienced Adonai yet, since the word of Adonai had not yet been revealed to him. **8** Adonai called Samuel again for the third time. So he got up and went to Eli, and said "Here I am, for you called me." Then Eli perceived that Adonai was calling the boy. **9** So Eli said to Samuel, "Go back to sleep, and if He calls you, say: 'Speak, Adonai, for Your servant is listening.'" So Samuel went back and lay down in his place. **10** Then Adonai came and stood and called as at the other times, "Samuel! Samuel!" Then Samuel said, "Speak, for Your servant is listening."

God has a special blessing for you. It might be hearing his voice like Samuel or Moses. It might be to become a great worshipper like David, a preacher like John, or like the Apostle Paul. Whatever Adonai's blessing for you may be, always remember the blessing is a gift. It is to be used to serve Him and to help others.

**PRACTICAL APPLICATIONS**

My Special Gift

### FOR CHILDREN 4-6 YEARS OLD

Parents, please read Psalm 119:153-176 as a reminder of God's commandments for your child/children.

**Parents:**

Parents write three blessings for your child/children. Together you can decorate it or put it in a frame to hang on his/her bedroom wall for him/her to declare every day.

### FOR CHILDREN 7-12 YEARS OLD

Pray and ask God to reveal the unique gift that he has blessed you with. Ask Him to teach you how to use your gift to help others.

Ask your parents to write three blessings for you. Together you can decorate it or put it in a frame to hang on your bedroom wall for you to declare every day.

Parents, please read Psalm 119:153-176 as a reminder of God's commandments for your child/children.

Children, please read three verses each night before bed from Psalm 119:153-176.

## FOLLOW-UP FROM THE LAST TORAH PORTION

Ask who wants to share from last week's practical application

## FOR CHILDREN 4-6 YEARS OLD

Parents, please read Psalm 119:129-152 as a reminder of God's commandments for your child/children.

## FOR CHILDREN 7-12 YEARS OLD

Parents, please read Psalm 119:129-152 as a reminder of God's commandments for your child/children.

Children, please read three verses each night before bed from Psalm 119:129-152. Then write two verses from the reading that ascribe greatness to Adonai. Study and memorize them.

# QUESTIONS - TEACHERS ANSWER KEY

1. **Which tribe was blessed to judge with the Urim and Thummim?**
   Levi

2. **Who is described as a lion's cub?**
   Dan

3. **Whose sons will be scattered to the nations of the earth?**
   Joseph

4. **Where did Moses die?**
   On Mount Nebo

5. **Where was he buried?**
   In the land of Moab

6. **How old was he when he died?**
   120 years old

7. **According to 2 Peter 1:3, what do we receive from Adonai?**
   Everything pertaining to life and Godliness

8. **Which tribe is blessed as a warrior to help his brothers?**
   Judah

9. **Which tribe is not mentioned by name in the blessing?**
   Simeon

10. <u>Issachar</u> rejoices in his tents with the abundance of the seas and hidden treasure of the sand. (Deuteronomy 33:19)

# QUESTIONS - CHILDREN'S COPY

1. Which tribe was blessed to judge with the Urim and Thummim?

2. Who is described as a lion's cub?

3. Whose sons will be scattered to the nations of the earth?

4. Where did Moses die?

5. Where was he buried?

6. How old was he when he died?

7. According to 2 Peter 1:3, what do we receive from Adonai?

8. Which tribe is blessed as a warrior to help his brothers?

9. Which tribe is not mentioned by name in the blessing?

10. _____rejoices in his tents with the abundance of the seas and hidden treasure of the sand. (Deuteronomy 33:19)

## CRAFTS SUPPLIES FOR THE TORAH PORTION VEZOT-HA'BRACHA

**SUPPLIES:**
1. "12×12" color Cardstock
2. Empty Toilet Rolls
3. Construction Paper
4. White Paper
5. Gems and Stickers
6. Gold Paint
7. Brushes
8. Popsicle Sticks
9. Glue
10. Glue sticks
11. Coloring supplies

# CRAFTS: TORAH SCROLL

1. Each child receives 2 toilet paper empty rolls. You can buy them on Amazon.
2. They will wrap the roll in blue paper and secure it with tape.

3. They will take white paper and tape it on each side as shown to make it look like an open scroll.
4. Paint popsicle sticks gold and allow them to dry.

5. They will decorate the rolls with gems and stickers.
6. Then they will glue the gold sticks as shown.

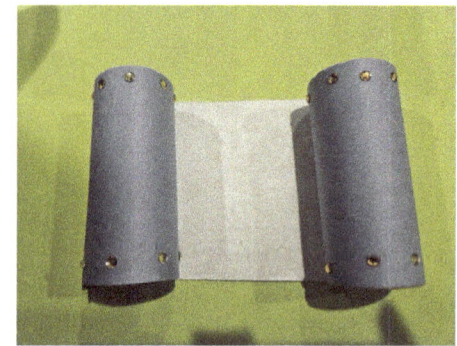 

7. With a glue stick, glue the paper with the Torah sign as shown.

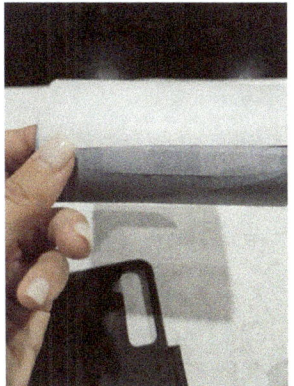 

8. In the 12×12" cardstock, make a 1" circle with a glue stick.
9. Attach the center of the white part of the scroll. You want to be able to open and close the scroll.
10. Color the Word of God sign and place it on top.

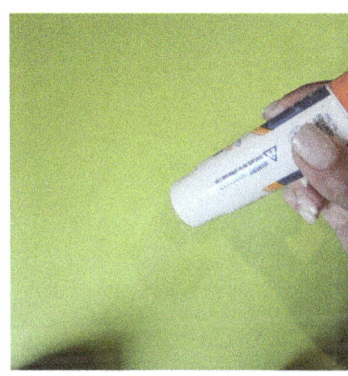 

THE FINISHED TORAH SCROLL

# About the Authors

**Natalee Henry** began her personal faith journey in 1996 with a burning desire to live an extraordinary life for the Lord. Since then, the Lord has kindled a passion within her for sharing and teaching the Word of God.

In 2016, God answered Natalee's prayer for spiritual growth when she was introduced to studying, learning, and implementing the Torah way of life as a believer in Yeshua. Natalee is a Torah-observant believer learning to honor God's Appointed Times and serving within her local congregation to all ages.

Natalee is an author, motivational speaker, and founder of the Season Destiny Ministry designed to *"**empower youths to make the right decisions in life.**"* Natalee is a graduate of International Seminary Bible College, and authored ***Seasons of Life-Taking Man Back To God***, 2005; ***Embracing Destiny***, 2010; ***Overcome to Fulfill Your Purpose: Become Successfully You, Successfully You, Leadership Training Workbook*** 2018, and her most recent book, ***Making Transition Through Crisis: A Rebuilding Guide for Young Professionals***, 2021.

Natalee has a passion for young people and seeks to share with them that they do not have to 'settle' for being less than God created them to be; nor do they need to succumb to today's culture, lies, and worldliness.

 **Yevgeniya Calendrillo** was born and raised in Ukraine to a secular Jewish family. Growing up, Yevgeniya yearned for a relationship with God for many years. By the age of 24, she was married and living in the United States. Yevgeniya and her husband are entrepreneurs and business partners selling their artwork and also are heavily focused on nutrition and health. Yevgeniya and her husband have one son, whom she homeschooled for 3 1/2 years.

Yevgeniya was invited to a Messianic congregation in Brooklyn where she accepted Yeshua as her Savior; and opened the Bible for the very first time. Yevgeniya has been a Messianic believer for over 20 years.

Yevgniya has a Bachelor's degree in Fashion Design from the Fashion Institute of Technology, New York. Yevgeniya has many years of experience in the New York fashion industry. Yevgniya is an artist who is gifted in watercolor painting. She recently discovered her talent for children's crafts and utilizes her knowledge, and experience in arts and design, as tools for investing in children for the Kingdom of God. Yevgeniya is currently serving as a Children's Ministry Leader and a children's Torah teacher at Save The Nations.

Yevgeniya has a passion to follow God, to be obedient to His Torah instructions, to seek Him diligently, and to walk in her calling to teach Torah and Hebrew lessons to children.

## About the Book

Shemott (Book 2: Exodus) is a part of the Torah Curriculum for children, covering the first five books of the Bible. This curriculum is based on the weekly Torah Portions so they may learn Torah in a simple and practical way.

The Lessons are structured so our children will learn from the Torah Portions and see the connection with Yeshua (Jesus), and the work of the Holy Spirit. Our aim is not just to give information but to teach Torah principles and demonstrate how to use them in their lives.

Each lesson is designed as a guide for teaching the Torah Portions to children ages 4 to 12 years. This curriculum is filled with creative crafts designed by Yevgeniya and insightful lessons written by Natalee.

**Visit our website at www.torah4children.net to learn more about other books from our curriculum and our ministry.**

# Other Books in the Curriculum

  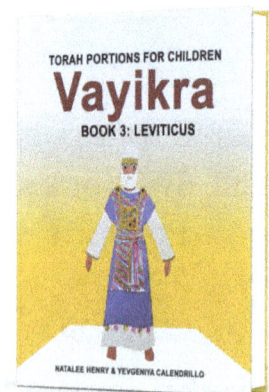 

We would love to hear your feedback about our curriculum. Please visit our website to share your comments. www.torah4children.net

Please help us spread the word. Please write us a review on Amazon and share any pictures you have taken while completing a lesson. We would greatly appreciate it.

Thank you so much for your attention and participation.

Natalee & Yevgeniya

www.ingramcontent.com/pod-product-compliance
Lightning Source LLC
Chambersburg PA
CBHW081331230426
43667CB00018B/2894